TRADITIONAL CHEESEMAKING

TRADITIONAL CHEESEMAKING

Josef Dubach

Translated by Bill Hogan

Intermediate Technology Publications *in association with*
the Swiss Centre for Appropriate Technology (SKAT) 1989

Published by Intermediate Technology Publications,
103-105 Southampton Row, London WC1B 4HH, UK.

© Intermediate Technology Publications 1989

ISBN 0 946688 43 5

Printed by the Russell Press Ltd., Bertrand Russell House, Gamble Street, Nottingham NG7 4ET, UK.

Contents

Illustrations

Preface

In the nineteenth century Swiss cheesemaking was an important factor in promoting rural development. Before the expansion of tourism, cattle grazing was the most appropriate method of land use in the higher valleys and the Alps; in many regions, for the peasants, it was the only alternative to emigration. However, milk production could only be increased where there was a market for this nutritious but highly perishable product. For the peasants of isolated valleys and Alps, cheesemaking was the only way to overcome this bottleneck. Thus, the peasants formed co-operatives which they initially ran themselves and, later on, rented out to specialized workmen who improved techniques and turned cheesemaking into a highly respected trade.

The better the cheese, the higher was the price it commanded in local and regional markets. As the demand for high quality cheese rose and export markets were opened, the dairies became able to pay more for the milk they used, and soon the peasants began to increase production by improving the quality of their livestock, pastures and stock farming techniques. By the beginning of the twentieth century, Emmentaler, Tilsiter, Gruyère, Appenzeller, and the cheeses from other relatively isolated valleys had become highly valued export products. This profitable trade was — and still is — a reliable source of income for thousands of cheesemakers and dairy farmers in Switzerland.

Similar strategies to achieve rural development have been adopted by French, Dutch, Danish, English and Italian farmers and cheesemakers, to mention only a few of the nations which have become famous for the quality of their cheese.

Based on this model of rural development, which, at home, proved to be a successful way of integrating isolated peasants into national and international markets and thereby stimulating their production and raising their incomes, the Swiss Development Corporation (SDC), a public agency for the promotion of social and economic development in the Third World, began to transfer cheesemaking techniques in order to generate similar processes of change in the peasant community of those poor countries which have a potential for dairy farming. The first project of this programme was set up in Langtang, Nepal, as early as 1954.

The production of cheese and yoghurt, mainly for the tourist market, soon became an important source of income for some small dairy farmers in the valleys of the Himalayas. In 1977 a similar project was set up in Afghanistan.

In Latin America, the programme was started in Peru in 1970. Initially, its main objective was to offer a productive alternative to the peasants of the Sheque valley near Lima, the capital of Peru. Later, in 1972, the Programme, in close collaboration with the Instituto de Investigaciones Agroindustrial now the Instituto Nacional de Desarrollo Agroindustrial (INDA) expanded its activities to many other regions of the Peruvian highlands. In 1981 the Instituto Nacional de Investigación y Promoción Agropecuaria (INIPA) became the most important national partner institution and the project soon became integrated into the Programa Nacional de Queserías, which still receives some limited follow-up assistance by SDC.

In Peru, the programme trained some 30 technicians and extension workers, who were specializing in small-scale cheesemaking, as well as about 200 peasants and workers from co-operatives and other forms of collective enterprises. Altogether it advised and promoted the establishment of more than 80 small rural cheese factories.

Based on a recommendation made by FAO, the programme initiated its activities in Ecuador in 1978. As suggested by the evaluation of the Peruvian experience, it co-operates not only with the Ministerio de Agricultura y Ganaderia, the official counterpart institution, but also with the Fondo Ecuatoriano Populorum Progressio (FEPP) and other non-governmental organizations interested in promoting rural development.

This joint effort allows for the application of a more integrated approach, according to which cheese manufacturing, as the main stimulant of change, should be accompanied by the promotion of peasant organizations, credit programmes, extension services for pasture, genetic and stock-farming improvements, as well as by the establishment of an association of peasant-owned cheese factories with its own marketing network and retail outlets. Also, the programme has given more importance to local demand and preferences. By adapting traditional techniques to produce suitably hygienic fresh cheese, which may be easily subsidized by profits from other types of dairy products, it is possible to improve the peasants' own diet and thus their conditions of health. Finally, cheesemaking should be complemented by other activities such as meat processing, as well as by biogas or solar energy programmes.

In such a strategy of integrated rural development the promotion of small-scale cheesemaking may become a key element in generating a series of positive spin-off effects. This concept cannot be adopted by all groups of peasants, but in general, at least the following conditions and arguments should be considered:

○ the peasants must be organized, well motivated and have some previous experience in stock-raising;

○ there must be enough land to expand and increase pastures without generating ecological problems;

○ the producers need access to credit and extension services to establish a small cheese factory and improve their livestock, pastures and farming techniques;

○ cheese production by small-holders should only be encouraged in isolated areas where climate and ecological conditions do not permit the production of food crops and where there is no alternative market for milk: to increase the consumption of freshly pasteurized milk is always a better way of improving the diet of the poor;

○ in the case of co-operative cheesemaking, additional assistance in management, accountancy and organization of self-help groups is indispensable;

○ in most developing countries, well-matured cheese is mainly consumed by the middle and upper classes who live in the major cities, markets to which the peasants usually have no direct access; unless they manage to establish their own marketing network, most of the value added by cheese production is therefore lost to the middlemen;

○ the general economic policies (milk price, import restrictions, credit availability to small farmers) and technical extension systems should encourage dairy production, and actively assist the peasants in their efforts to raise their output.

The present handbook summarizes the author's experience gained during the 30 years which he and other experts of SDC have spent in different developing countries promoting appropriate techniques for cheesemaking as a means of improving peasant livelihood. The book is now published in English to assist organized groups of small producers as well as governmental and non-governmental institutions which promote rural development in Third World countries.

F.R. Staehelin
Director
Swiss Development Co-operation

Introduction

Why make cheese?

There are many remote areas scattered throughout the world where dairy farming is a well-established occupation. Large quantities of high-grade milk can be produced in such areas but the local market cannot always absorb them, especially during peak periods. Converting milk to cheese is one method of dealing with the surplus. Cheesemaking provides an incentive for improving dairying as well as creating new jobs. It also improves the local diet and raises the standard of living generally, through a better understanding of hygiene, scientific techniques and community spirit. In a Third World setting, the local cheese plant often serves as a centre for community activities.

Nutritionally, cheese resembles meat but it is a more concentrated food. It contains large quantities of protein, fat and minerals and is rich in phosphorus and calcium which are both beneficial to growing children.

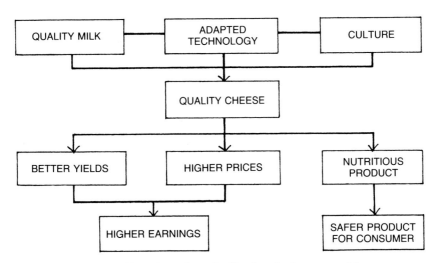

Figure 1. The 'knock-on' effects of cheesemaking.

1

If rural cheese factories are organized as co-operatives or associations then the entire community will benefit. As members of a co-operative, dairy farmers who send their milk to the plant will have a stake in its development and future success. With a higher income, farmers can improve their herds, pastures, and dairy practices, and high quality cheese and butter will contribute towards a healthier national diet. But whatever structure the rural cheese factory adopts — whether as a co-operative or as a private concern — there is a 'knock on' effect which will be to everyone's advantage (see Figure 1).

Hygiene in both the cheese factory and the milking parlour is clearly vital. Cheesemakers must be trained to make products of the highest quality, so as never to put the consumer's health at risk. They must be able to solve the many problems which may arise during processing, and personnel must be trained to work conscientiously in constructing, equipping, organizing and administering the enterprise.

Location

There are several factors to be considered before deciding on the best location for a cheese factory. Due to production costs, cheese protein is more expensive than meat protein. It is advisable, therefore, to locate cheese factories in remote areas where milk distribution costs are high and demands are low. Siting cheese factories in heavily populated urban areas is less important, as fresh milk can be transported easily and cheaply and is always in demand, especially by children for whom it is a better source of nutrition than cheese.

In remote areas, cheesemaking can be the best way to overcome the problem of milk overproduction. By converting milk into cheese during periods of peak production, its nutritional value can be conserved and stored until needed, although it should be remembered that cheese cannot be kept forever, under normal circumstances. Economically, rural rather than urban locations are more suitable for cheese factories.

Traditional cheesemaking has a definite role to play throughout the world. In the Third World, many rural cheese factories are already in full operation and are producing a whole range of high-quality products. The fine cheeses of Europe are the result of hundreds of years of labour and research. Good cheesemakers must be willing to experiment and innovate to achieve the best results. Although cheese is usually made from cows' milk, every kind of milk can be employed. Excellent cheeses are made from goats' and ewes' milk. In Asia, yak and buffalo milk are used. Cheesemakers will often strive to imitate a well-known European cheese such as Gouda or Cheddar, but local conditions and national preferences will soon exert their influences and new types of cheese will emerge to suit local preferences.

2

International cheeses and cheesemaking

In the Himalayan area of Central Asia cheese is made from skimmed milk curds which are first acidified then stretched into thin strips by hand and left to dry on the roof until sufficiently hard. This type of cheese lasts for months and provides a reserve of food in winter.

In the Near East, the Bedouins make cheese from whole milk heated to approximately 80°C, then acidified with lemon juice to coagulate it. The whey is drained off and the curd pressed in straw baskets. When stored in brine, this type of cheese keeps for many months and will not be damaged by the desert heat.

France produces many soft variety names, the most famous of which are Camembert and Brie. Switzerland and Germany have produced Emmental and Gruyère for several hundred years, often in co-operatives. Renowned for their great size, they can weigh up to 110kg. They have a hard consistency and an elastic texture with typical eyes of 1 to 2 cm diameter. Cheese is one of Switzerland's principal exports.

The UK, Australia, New Zealand, Canada and the United States all make cheese in large dairies, of which cheddar is the best-known variety. Holland produces Edam and Gouda and Denmark's main cheese is Danbo. Italy is famous for Parmesan, a cheese which requires prolonged storage for full maturation to produce its characteristic flavour.

A word of warning

For those deciding to establish a rural cheese production facility, patience and perseverance must be the key factors. Good hygiene both on a personal level and in the work environment is essential. Flexibility and good working relationships are desirable if top-quality products are to be obtained. Cheeses which are suspect or of inferior quality must not be released for sale to the public. These downgraded products can often be sold to large cheese factories for processing. Cheesemaking requires a balance of skill and technology, theory and good business practice which all combine to create top-quality speciality products that are highly desirable to the consumer.

The cheesemaking process described later in this book has been developed without the use of preservatives — neither in the milk nor in the cheese. For this reason, cheese produced in this way will have a shorter shelf-life than other cheeses containing preservatives.

Basic cheesemaking principles

Cheese is milk curd — a substance formed from the coagulation of milk by rennet and acid — separated from the whey and pressed or moulded into a solid mass. It contains concentrated milk solids, water, rennet (to coagulate the milk), bacterial cultures (to acidify the milk and curds and produce desirable characteristics), salt, and, sometimes, calcium chloride. The calcium chloride is necessary in order to compensate for the loss of the free calcium in the milk resulting from the pasteurization process.

Cheesemaking equipment and methods vary but the basic principles have remained unchanged for thousands of years:
1. Milking
2. Coagulation
3. Separation of curds and whey
4. Forming the curd into a cheese mould
5. Salting for conservation and flavour
6. Maturation and conservation.

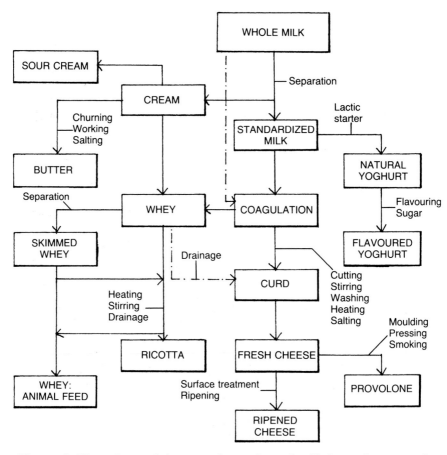

Figure 2. Flow chart of the transformation of milk into cheese and its by-products.

4

Figure 3. The cheesemaking process.

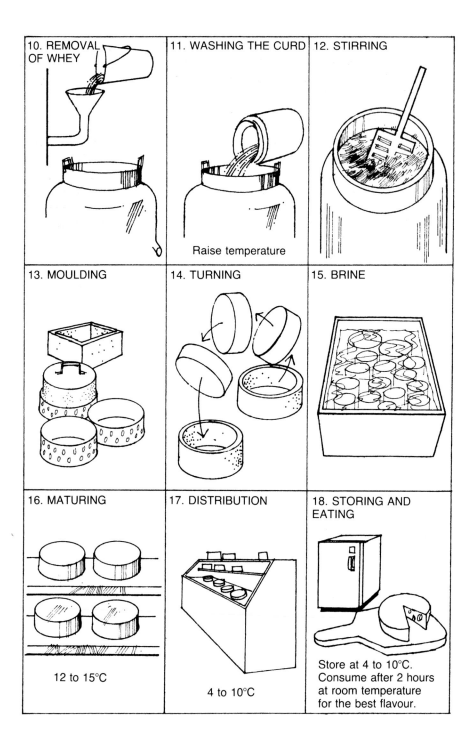

10. REMOVAL OF WHEY

11. WASHING THE CURD

Raise temperature

12. STIRRING

13. MOULDING

14. TURNING

15. BRINE

16. MATURING

12 to 15°C

17. DISTRIBUTION

4 to 10°C

18. STORING AND EATING

Store at 4 to 10°C.
Consume after 2 hours
at room temperature
for the best flavour.

Traditionally salt was used in cheesemaking in order to preserve the product for a longer period. However, today conservation can be achieved by the use of lactic cultures, so that over-salting is no longer necessary.

The stages involved in the modern preparation of cheese are illustrated in Figure 3.

The various stages of cheesemaking are described in detail in Part II of this book. Part I covers aspects of hygiene and basic microbiology, an elementary knowledge of which is required in order to appreciate the biochemical processes involved during processing. Part III deals with other products that may be produced from milk, and includes a section describing the construction of and equipment requirements for the preparation of cheese.

Part I
Bacteria

Bacteria are microscopic one-cell organisms. Each cell is surrounded by a wall which characterizes the shape of the bacterium. Bacterial shape is an important aid to classification which may be done under the microscope. The cell may be spherical (coccus) or rod-shaped (bacillus) and of varying lengths and diameter.

Bacteria multiply by the simple method of binary division: each cell grows to a critical size and then divides to produce two cells with identical properties. Each cell will subsequently grow and divide at about the same rate as the parent cell. This chain of events will continue until limited by the exhaustion of required nutrients or by accumulation of toxic substances.

Bacteria may be found everywhere — on land, in the air, in water, and most bacteria are non-pathogenic. Bacteria are therefore commonly found on the surface of, or in, various food products, such as milk. Even if the milk is obtained under reasonably hygienic conditions and from healthy cows, it always contains some bacteria which, under certain conditions, can multiply within a few hours so that the milk can become unfit for either cheesemaking or drinking. Adequate milk pasteurization (or other heat treatments) will ensure adequate destruction of known pathogens without destroying or affecting to any significant extent the valuable components of milk. The surviving heat-resistant organisms are not of any danger. Pasteurized milk can however be contaminated with all types of micro-organisms.

However, some bacteria such as *streptococcus lactis*, when growing in milk, convert the milk sugar (lactose) into lactic acid, an essential ingredient in traditional cheesemaking. Other types of bacteria found in milk and cheese include monococcus, diplococcus, tetracoccus, streptococcus, staphilococcus, lactobacillus and bacterias propionicas.

Factors affecting the survival of bacteria

Temperature

For each kind of bacteria there is an ideal temperature for maximum growth and reproduction. Some prefer a relatively cool environment

8

(between 5°C and 15°C) while others will grow at temperatures of up to 55°C. Lactic acid-producing bacteria commonly multiply best in temperatures similar to the animal's body temperature. For this reason, untreated milk in churns and tanks that are left or transported in the heat can arrive at the cheese plant with high levels of lactic acid and low levels of lactose. In the production of hard cheese bacteria which can withstand high temperatures (thermophiles) are added. These include *Streptococcus thermophilus*, *Lactobacillus helveticus* and propionibacteria.

Each kind of bacteria also has a minimum and maximum temperature within which it can live and multiply, and below or above which it cannot grow. Between 5°C and 10°C, lactic acid-producing bacteria slow down their reproduction rate considerably and so reduce the conversion rate of lactose into lactic acid. Propionic bacteria develop at temperatures over 18°C when they consume lactic acid, producing CO_2 and propionic acid, leading to the sweetish flavour and 'eye' formation in Emmental and Gruyère cheeses. When the eyes are well developed the fermentation can be stopped by lowering the store room temperature. Milk stored below 5° does not sour quickly and therefore keeps much longer than warm milk; below 0°C bacteria remain dormant, although they do not die. In addition to specific temperatures for pasteurization, temperature control at each stage of the cheesemaking process is vital (see Table).

Temperature control in cheesemaking.

	Temperature (°C)
Milking	37.5
Cooling	below 15
Transport to factory	18
Reception at factory	20
Pasteurization (30 minutes)	65
Acidification and coagulation	33
Preparation of culture	22
Stirring	35 to 38
Moulding	20
Brine and maturing (neutralization of acid)	12 to 14

Acidity

As with temperature, each kind of bacteria prefers a certain level of acidity. Microbes which cause putrifaction and destroy food cannot survive an acid environment. So if cheese and butter contain enough lactic acid produced by bacterial fermentation (*Streptococcus lactis* for example), they will last for longer. However, when acid levels get too high the bacteria are inhibited; also, too acid a taste will not please the consumer.

Disinfectant

A cheese factory should be cleaned first then disinfected with hot water or a chlorine-based substance. All milk churns, tanks, and cheesemaking equipment must be washed, disinfected and rinsed with clean water, preferably tap or running water, and strict hygiene must be observed at all times (see box).

The importance of hygiene
- Hygienic milking practices
- Do not use cloth filters to strain the milk
- Do not dilute milk with water
- Do not mix old and new milk
- Cleanliness in the cheese factory
- High quality cultures
- Cleanliness of the separation and moulding equipment
- Daily cleaning of whey tank
- Keep pigs away from dairy

Antibiotics and other inhibitary substances

Antibiotics are medicines which kill certain micro-organisms and are used to cure both man and animals of infectious diseases. The lactic bacteria, which produce lactic acid in milk, yoghurt, cultures, and cheeses, are very sensitive to antibiotics such as penicillin. For this reason, milk from cows which were treated with penicillin is not suitable for cheesemaking, since the antibiotics do not permit the growth of bacteria which is important for the fermentation in the cheese. The absence of lactic acid allows the coliforms to increase and produce gases which cause swelling of the cheese. Such milk containing antibiotics must not be used, since even a small quantity can ruin the processing of all of the cheese and butter, in fact it is advisable not to use this milk in any foods destined for human consumption.

Bacteriophage

During the author's twenty years of activity in rural cheese factories, problems caused by bacteriophages have never been detected.

Bacteriophages are viruses that are pathogenic to bacteria, affecting above all the streptococcus of lactic cultures. The multiplication of bacteriophage can be so great that they can destroy the acidifying culture overnight.

1. During hand milking some micro-organisms enter the milk but with machine milking propionic starters must be added.

2. For hard cheese a mixed culture of thermophiles (heat-resistant bacteria) is added.

3. Heating cheese to 53°C reduces harmful bacteria and gives a hard texture.

4. After 24 hours in the press the lactose is transformed into lactic acid.

5. Brining develops the rind which helps the cheese to keep its form and preserves the flavour.

6. Propionic bacteria produce CO_2 and propionic acid, leading to the 'eye' formation in Emmental and Gruyère cheeses.

Figure 4. Propionic acid fermentation of 'Swiss' cheese.

11

It seems that the bacteriophage may only be present in factories using sophisticated processing methods. Therefore, those in charge of rural cheese factories should not waste time trying to hunt down the bacteriophage, since there are many other less complex causes of fluctuations in the acidification of lactic cultures, milk and cheese.

Bacteria in cheese

Cheeses do not normally carry disease-producing organisms because its level of acidity, lack of oxygen and low moisture content, combined with bacteriocidal agents such as salt, all combine to prevent the survival and reproduction of pathogens. However, if the cheese has been poorly made and has a low level of lactic acid, or if it is marketed too soon, some harmful organisms may survive. In the USA, many states have laws that if cheese is made from unpasteurized milk it should be held in a cheese store for more than 60 days, at a temperature not lower than 8°C.

Part II
From milk to cheese

Chapter 1
Milk

Definition and composition

Fresh milk is a white liquid, with an agreeable odour and a faintly sweet taste, produced by female mammals to feed their offspring. Humans use cows' milk as well as buffaloes', goats', sheep and mares' milk, either to drink directly or to make into different foods, such as cheese, butter, cream and yoghurt.

Seven-eighths of milk is water, with solids — the nutritious part — forming the remaining one-eighth. The solids can be broken down approximately as follows (see also Table):

Lactose		4.8%
Fat		4.0%
Protein	Casein 2.8% Whey proteins 0.7%	3.5%
Mineral salts		0.7%
		13.0%

One hundred kg of milk contains approximately 87kg or litres of pure water and 13kg of solids.

Milk production

Several factors affect the quality of milk, and to obtain the high-quality clean milk necessary for cheesemaking particular attention must be paid to the animals' diet and health and to the standard of hygiene in the milking parlour.

Diet

The following are all suitable as animal feed but may affect the colour, taste or smell of the milk in different ways:
○ Natural or artificial pasture (gives a yellow butterfat due to the presence of Beta Carotene — Vitamin A)

13

○ Hay (gives a white butterfat and a rather colourless butter)
○ Silage (which is not suitable for hard cheese)
○ Fresh meal, especially if mixed with molasses.

Milk: a balanced food.

	A 10-year-old child's daily requirement	Half a litre of milk contains	Percentage of daily requirement
Protein	90g	17g	19
Fat	90g	18g	20
Carbohydrate	325g	23.5g	7
Calories	2,550Kcal	340Kcal	13
Minerals			
Potassium	0.95g	0.81g	85
Calcium	1.75g	0.60g	34
Phosphorus	1.50g	0.41g	27
Trace elements			
Iodine	0.15g	0.02mg	13
Zinc	6.0mg	1.9mg	32
Vitamins			
B2	1.95mg	0.9mg	46
B12	0.005mg	0.003mg	60
C	75.00mg	8.5mg	11

Health

Milk must not be used for cheesemaking if the animal is diseased or sick in any way and care must be taken to prevent the following:
○ Aftosis (foot-and-mouth disease)
○ Brucellosis or undulant fever: (*brucella abortus* in bovines and *brucella melitensis* in goats)
○ Mastitis
○ Tuberculosis.

Milk must also be excluded from cheesemaking if it shows any chemical or physical abnormality, for example:
○ If the milk contains colostrum (until the sixth day after the birth)
○ If the milk contains antibiotics (until five full days after the last injection)
○ If the animal has been vaccinated within the previous 24 hours
○ If the milk has an abnormal flavour or aroma
○ If the milk has an abnormal colour, for example bloody.
○ If the milk is contaminated (with, for instance, dung, cattle feed or sediment).

The milking procedure

Before milking

○ Clean and disinfect the milking parlour (this should have a hard floor that can be cleaned after each milking).
○ Brush off the animal's flanks if they are dirty.
○ Wash all utensils with a good dairy disinfectant and rinse with clean water.
○ Wash the udder with lukewarm water and disinfect with a cloth used for this and no other purpose.
○ Wash and disinfect the milker's hands.
○ Control mastitis. This disease will destroy the udder and produces an abnormal milk.
○ Ensure that all milkers and cheesemakers are clean and healthy.

After milking

○ Wash all utensils immediately after use and keep them in a clean place.
○ Cool the milk to at least 15°C.
It is also important to remember the following:
○ In hand milking do not give the last milk to calves because it contains the highest proportion of fat. Instead, milk three teats completely and leave the fourth for the calf.
○ Never mix new milk with old.
○ Don't use cloth filters because they are very difficult to clean and may contaminate the milk.
○ Don't use milk buckets for other purposes.
○ Don't use rusty or oxidized churns or equipment.
○ Don't leave milk churns or receptacles full of water.
○ Send milk destined for cheesemaking to the cheese factory or dairy immediately after milking to prevent bacterial spoilage.
○ Wash, scrub well and rinse all equipment daily with hot water, detergents and a dairy disinfectant.

Mastitis detection (California mastitis test)

This test determines the presence or absence of leucocytes (pus indicating infection) in milk. There is a close relation between the number of leucocytes present in the sample and the degree of reaction.

Equipment

A pallet with four small numbered receiving dishes (Figure 5).
A narrow-necked plastic measuring bottle containing reagent. (A suitable reagent is one resazurin tablet and one rennet tablet dissolved in 50ml distilled water.)

Figure 5. Testing for mastitis.

Method

1. Extract a few squirts of milk from each teat into the corresponding dish in the pallet (Figure 5).
2. Tilt the pallet to one side to equalize the amount of milk in each dish, leaving about 2 ml in each.
3. Add the same amount of reagent to each dish according to instructions.
4. Gently agitate the pallet to mix the milk and reagent. Wait for 30 to 60 seconds and observe the results.

Results

Normal milk: The milk does not congeal and its colour does not change.

Slightly infected milk: Small clots will form, the milk will thicken very slightly and the colour will darken. (The colour produced will vary according to the type of reagent used.)

Heavily infected milk: The milk will become very thick and dark.

Recommendations

Slightly infected milk should be separated from healthy milk and pasteurized before use. Antibiotics are not necessarily recommended for light cases of mastitis; improved dairy hygiene and frequent strip milking should be sufficient to cure these cases.

Heavily infected milk should never be used for cheesemaking and must be kept completely separate from good milk. It should be boiled and used as calf feed. In serious cases of mastitis it is advisable to consult a vet.

Precautions should be taken in all cases of mastitis not to spread the

16

infection from affected animals to healthy ones through hands, towels and milking machines. Apart from special attention to hygiene, affected cows should be milked last. If a milking machine is used, a re-usable, cheap, in-line filter can be used to detect mastitis, which shows up on a fine screen as small lumps or particles.

Reception

Milk should arrive at the cheese factory as soon as possible after milking to prevent excessive acid development; too high a level of acidity will damage the cheese. The milk should be received and weighed outside the plant to avoid suppliers having to enter the building and so prevent possible contamination. As all equipment for transporting and holding milk must be washed with hot water and a good dairy detergent and rinsed immediately, facilities for this should be provided in the reception area.

Analysis

A series of tests determine the milk quality and ensure that the milk is pure, clean and suitable for cheesemaking. The main tests are:

Sensory analysis

○ Odour — free from acidity and containing no foreign substances.
○ Taste — normal or strange?
○ Appearance — colour and consistency.

Laboratory tests

○ Bacteriological
○ Physio-chemical
  — titration of acidity
  — percentage of fat
  — density of milk
  — control of impurities

Reductase Test

This test, based on the speed with which milk changes colour as a result of the reaction between methylene blue (methylthionine chloride) and bacteria, indicates the level of bacteria in the milk.

Equipment and reagents

Reductase tube approximately 25ml capacity, ringed at 10ml
A jug for the sample
A 37°C incubator, with test tube

A 1ml pipette
Methylene blue
All equipment must be sterilized.

Method

1. Cool 200ml of distilled water to 40°C.
2. Add one tablet of methylene blue and let it dissolve completely. (Keep this solution in a dark bottle and do not expose it to light.) Note: Since methods differ from country to country, it is advisable to follow the instructions of the producer of methylene blue solution.
3. Pour 10 ml of milk into each test tube.
4. Add 1 ml of methylene blue solution to each test tube.
5. Agitate the tubes to mix the solution with the milk.
6. Place the test tubes in the incubator at 37° to 38°C and check them every hour.

Results

If two-thirds or more of the milk in a test tube becomes discoloured in less than the acceptable time given below, it should be rejected.

Time	Level of bacteria	Quality of milk
after 5 hours	very low	very good
3 to 5 hours	low	good
2 to 3 hours	medium	acceptable
1 to 2 hours	high	bad
less than 1 hour	very high	unacceptable

Recommendations

Milk which discolours before two hours should not be used and indicates a lack of hygiene in its production: badly washed churns and milking equipment, improper cooling temperatures or impure water favouring the growth of undesirable micro-organisms.

Acidity determination

The level of acidity in milk relates to its microbiological content and therefore can indicate its purity and freshness. It can also be used to calculate the effectiveness of the lactic cultures being used in the cheese plant and the time required to reach desired levels of acidification.

Equipment and reagents

A clear flask
An eye-dropper

18

An acidimeter
A 10ml milk pipette
A one-tenth solution of sodium hydroxide (Na0H)
An indicator solution of phenolphthalein in 2 per cent alcohol

Method

1. Add 9ml of the milk to the flask.
2. Add three or four drops of phenolphthalein.
3. Fill the burette of the acidimeter with the solution of Na0H and begin to titrate the milk in the flask. The titration is complete when the milk turns pink and remains so for at least 10 seconds.

Result

The acidity in ° Dornic is equal to the number of 0.10ml of Na0H used.

Recommendations

Fresh milk should normally have a reading of between 16° and 18° Dornic. In remote mountainous areas, however, readings of up to 20° Dornic, resulting from long trips over mountain passes often on mule or horseback, are acceptable. If the milk has an acid level of more than 20 to 21° Dornic, 6 to 10 per cent of *clean* water may be added, as soon as the milk arrives at the cheese factory, in order to reduce the acidity.

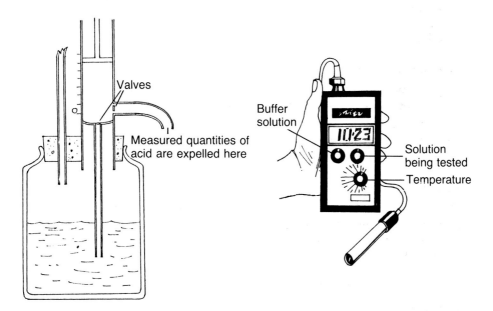

Figure 6. An acidimeter.   **Figure 7. A pH meter.**

pH meters

Some cheesemakers prefer pH meters (Figure 7) to the more traditional acidimeters, as they give faster and more accurate results and are much easier to use.

Readings should be taken of the pH of the milk before the starter is added, of the starter itself and throughout the cheesemaking process since this can help maintain consistency and prevent errors.

Readings vary according to the type of cheese being made and local conditions but, once requirements are established, the pH meter is an excellent instrument for helping to produce a reasonably standard product. pH meters are available in a wide variety of sizes: a stick pH meter would be adequate for a small plant but a built-in system is advisable in a larger factory.

Some meters come with a digital read-out and special buffer solutions of known pH value to calibrate them; however, pH electrodes are very fragile.

Test for antibiotics

Method

Inoculate 10ml of milk suspected of containing antibiotics with one tenth ml of starter culture and incubate at 32°C for five hours. Measure the level of acidity.

Result

There will be little or no increase in acidity if the milk contains antibiotics (or other inhibitory substances).

Equipment and reagents

Gerber butyrometers with tops
Gerber centrifuge (manual or electric) of 1,000 to 1,200 rpm
Special milk pipettes of 11ml capacity
10ml unbreakable pipettes (for sulphuric acid)
Water bath (65°C)
Sulphuric acid (H_2SO_4) at a relative density of 1.820 to 1.825
Amyl alcohol

Method

It must be emphasized that great care must be taken with this test, as it involves the use of sulphuric acid.
1. Put 10ml of sulphuric acid in the butyrometer.
2. Add 11ml of milk, taking care that it runs down the side of the

butyrometer so as not to mix too quickly with the acid and burn the milk solids.

3. Add 1ml of amyl alcohol to the mixture.
4. Put the top tightly on the butyrometer and agitate until the solution is well mixed.
5. Place the butyrometer in the centrifuge and leave it in motion for approximately five minutes.
6. Remove the butyrometers and place them in a water bath at 65°C for three or four minutes. Read the level of fat in the butyrometer.

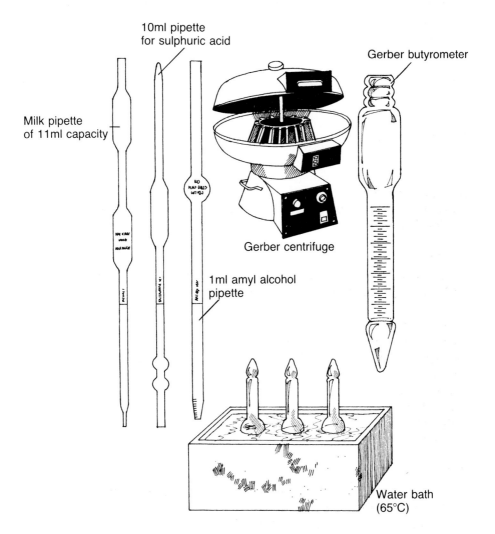

Figure 8. Equipment for testing fat content.

21

Recommendations

The normal fat level of milk depends on several different factors but should in any case not be below three per cent.

Factors affecting fat content		Fat content
Breed	Brown Swiss	4%
	Jersey	5%
	Holstein	3%
Lactation	first months	low
	last months	high
Milking	first milking	2%
	last milking	4.5%*
	average	3.25%

*For this reason the calf should not be given the last milk.

Density determination

This simple test to determine milk density reveals whether or not the milk has been diluted. Although density varies considerably in milk from different animals and breeds, the following table gives an indication of relative densities:

Relative density and composition in normal, watered and skimmed milk.

	Relative density	Fat	Non-fat solids	Total solids
Normal milk	1.028-1.033	3% min	8.5% min	11.5% min
Watered milk	1.025	lower	lower	lower
Skimmed milk	1.035	lower	same	lower
Double fraud*	1.030	much lower	lower	lower

*Milk which has been both skimmed and watered. As the density is the same as that for normal milk the fraud can only be detected with a fat test.

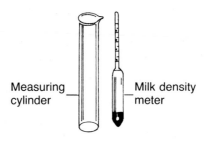

Measuring cylinder — Milk density meter

Figure 9. Measuring the density of milk.

22

Equipment

Jug
Thermometer
500cc measuring cylinder
Milk density meter, calibrated at 15°C (Scale: 22 to 36 = 1.022-1.036)

Method

1. Pour 500cc of milk sample down the inside of the measuring cylinder without making it bubble.
2. Gently place the milk density meter in the cylinder and let it float. It will rise to give a reading at the surface of the sample.

Temperature correction

For each degree above 15°C add 0.2 to the relative density. For each degree below 15°C subtract 0.2. For example, if the milk density meter shows a reading of 28 at a temperature of 25°C, then the corrected density reading is:

$$28 + (10 \times 0.2) = 30$$

Calculation of non-fat solids (Richmond's formula)

0.22 × percentage fat + 0.25 × specific gravity (corrected to 20°C) + 0.72 = percentage non-fat solids

Non-fat solids in normal milk fluctuate between 8.5 and 9 per cent. If the results are lower the milk is probably diluted.

Pasteurization

Even when hygienically produced and stored, milk can contain high levels of micro-organisms. Drinking untreated milk can cause gastric distress and more serious ailments such as brucellosis, tuberculosis and typhoid. If the animal is also dirty or unhealthy then the health risk is even greater.

Heat destroys the bacteria in milk and many people boil milk before drinking it to avoid illness. But boiling milk adversely affects proteins: some proteins may be denatured, and some lactose may be converted into caramel and burned milk has an unpleasant flavour and smell.

Pasteurizing milk avoids these problems. The milk is heated to a temperature well below boiling point for a prescribed period sufficient to eliminate harmful bacteria, but not enough to destroy the flavour or nutritive value.

23

Method

Filter the milk and run it into the cheese vat. Heat it either to 63°C for 30 minutes, to 68°C for 15 minutes (as practised in Ecuador) or 73°C for 15 seconds. Using cold water in the double-walled vat, cool the milk to the temperature needed for its coagulation (see p.73).

Cheese from unpasteurized milk

Although most factories in America and Europe now use pasteurized milk for drinking and cheesemaking, there are still several types of cheese made from unpasteurized milk. Gruyère and Emmental, for example, are made in Switzerland, France, Germany and Austria from traditional formulae using unpasteurized milk. Other cheeses are also made from unpasteurized milk, not to keep costs down but to obtain a distinctive flavour. Cheese made from unpasteurized milk clearly demands a far higher level of hygiene than cheese made from pasteurized milk. The strictest standards, from the condition of the dairy herd to the final steps in the cheesemaking process, must be rigidly adhered to when unpasteurized milk is used.

Cultures

The dairy culture contains micro-organisms useful for the manufacture of cheese and butter. Generally there are two types of coexisting micro-organisms. One type produce lactic acid from lactose and for that reason are called acidifiers, while the other type make substances with aroma and flavour and have been named aromatizers. The first type of micro-organisms ensure the presence of acid in the cheese and butter, thus prolonging the conservation time for these products since high acidity does not permit putrefying micro-organisms to live. The second type of micro-organisms produce a pleasant odour and flavour in both products, improving their quality and therefore increasing their sale price. The most commonly used culture in rural cheese factories is known as lactic culture, since its principle function is to form lactic acid from the lactose of the milk.

Mother-and-daughter solutions

A lactic culture can be initially propagated from a *liophilized* (freeze dried) powder form of the culture. When added to sterilized milk the acidifying and flavour-producing bacteria in the powder (see Figure 11) begin to multiply, producing an acid flavour and a pleasant odour. The milk coagulates, ideally forming a smooth white, gelatinous mass without cracks, grains or bubbles and with very little whey, containing an acidity level of 70 to 80° Dornic. This first propagation is known as the mother solution. Second and subsequent propagations are known as

Starter culture	Propagation duration

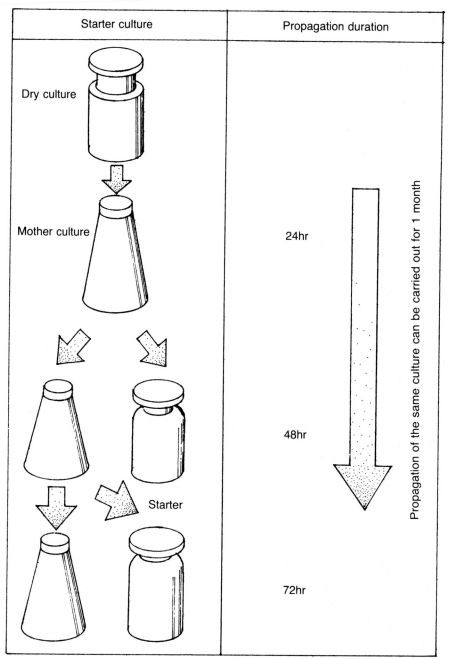

Dry culture

Mother culture   24hr

                        48hr

Starter

                        72hr

Propagation of the same culture can be carried out for 1 month

Figure 10. Mother and daughter solutions.*

*It is better to have a selection of non-bacteriaphage-related cultures and to rotate a selection of these cultures to minimize phage growth.

25

daughter solutions. The first daughter solution is made by mixing a small amount (2 per cent) of the mother solution with sterilized milk, and the second daughter solution is formed from the first daughter solution and so on successively.

A fresh solution should be made every day, or at least every other day, and in favourable conditions a lactic culture should last for a month (see Figure 10).

It is essential to observe careful hygiene with each propagation, both to eliminate any bacteria that the milk might contain and to prevent contamination. It is also important to use antibiotic-free milk (see p.10).

Propagating the mother solution

1. Put a heat-resistant funnel and bottle into a suitable volume of clean water in an appropriate container. (Glass may be used but care must be taken to cool and heat them slowly to prevent shattering.) Fill the bottle completely with water and ensure that air bubbles, which may contain bacteria that would survive the boiling, are excluded. Boil the water for 30 minutes, making sure that the bottle is completely submerged throughout the sterilizing procedure.
2. Put one or two litres of fresh antibiotic-free milk in a small, clean, three-litre pan. Cover the pan well and bring the milk to the boil, stirring occasionally with a pre-sterilized spoon to prevent milk solids sticking and burning. As soon as the milk boils fully, lower the heat to prevent it from boiling over. Never blow on the pan to prevent the milk from boiling over as this will contaminate it. Boil the milk over a low heat for 15 minutes. NB: It is better to sterilize the bottle, funnel and milk at the same time, using two pans, but if only one pan is used, boil the water first.
3. Carefully fill the bottle with the boiled milk, using the funnel. Seal the bottle with a hermetic top immediately and let it cool for a few minutes before submerging it in cold water. Keep the boiled water for the incubation tank.
4. Cool the milk to between 25°C and 30°C in a bath of stirred water. Do not open the bottle to take the temperature, as this will expose the milk to potential contamination. Instead, take the temperature of the water immediately surrounding the bottle.
5. Open the bottle, vial or packet of powdered culture near an open flame to help eliminate airborne microbes (some skill in microbiology is required). Open the bottle of sterilized milk, add the powdered culture and agitate the bottle so that the milk and powder are thoroughly mixed. Plug the bottle with sterilized cotton wool.
6. Put the bottle of inoculated milk in a water-bath at 20°C to 23°C (not less than 20°C) and place it in an incubator. Ensure that the temperature of the water in the water-bath remains constant

throughout the fermentation process and agitate the bottle occasionally for the first few hours to prevent the powder settling at the bottom of the bottle.

7. The bacteria in the mother solution take several hours to adapt to their new environment and incubation can take about 16 to 18 hours. After this time the population is high and in its final growth phase. If the solution is left in the incubator for longer it can become too acid and will coagulate, with the whey separating out. Some coagulation is normal: 0.6 or 0.7 per cent lactic acid is sufficient for milk to begin to coagulate. If carried too far the bacteria will die or degenerate and the culture will be useless (see Figure 11). It is important, therefore, to stop the incubation before the whey begins to separate. Skim the solution as it contains a very few lactic bacteria.

8. The solution should be used quickly or it will lose some strength. If it is not to be used immediately then it must be covered to prevent contamination by moulds, and cooled in a refrigerator to slow down bacterial growth. Cultures must not be kept in the curing room where there is a risk they will be contaminated by the many microbes present.

Propagating the daughter solution

Propagating the daughter solution is an almost identical process, but as the bacteria are already accustomed to the milk there is no phase of adaptation and they begin to multiply more quickly. Put some milk at a temperature of 20 to 23°C in the bottle, add some of the mother solution (1 to 2 per cent of the total milk), agitate them near an open flame and then fill the bottle with the remaining sterilized milk. A daughter solution needs to be incubated for only 12 to 16 hours but incubation conditions should otherwise be the same as for the mother solution.

Points to remember

○ Keep the culture (1 litre) separated from the large starter container (5 litres).

○ Whenever the mother culture shows signs of deterioration or insufficient growth it must be discarded and a new mother culture established from the dry starter culture powder.

○ Propagate the mother culture and the starter every day, or at least every other day.

○ Renew the culture at regular intervals. Sometimes a mother culture loses its desirable properties after two weeks, but will usually last for a month. It is always advisable to have a fresh dry culture in the refrigerator for speedy use.

○ Starter cultures are available, in a concentrated form, which require no preparation at all and which can be added directly to the cheese vat. These are available in deep-frozen or freeze-dried forms; the latter is ideal for a small-scale operation, or for use in an emergency.

A The bacteria adapt to the new environment, as when a new culture is prepared.

B The bacteria, having adapted to the milk, use the lactose and produce lactic acid. Their population increases rapidly and the milk thickens.

C As the amount of lactose available decreases and the milk becomes acidified bacterial growth diminishes and bacteria lack the ability to reproduce.

D The lack of lactose and oxygen and the excessive acidity produced by the bacteria themselves cause their degeneration and death.

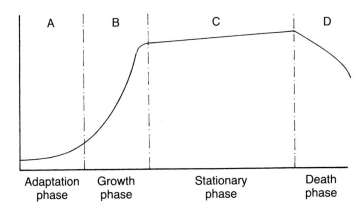

Figure 11. Development of lactic bacteria in milk.

Maturation of the milk

When the milk in the vat has reached the coagulation temperature, the lactic culture is added in the proportion of one litre per 100 litres of milk. The purpose for this procedure is to allow for the production of lactic acid from the lactose of the milk due to the action of the micro-organisms of the lactic culture. It is necessary for the milk to reach an optimum acidity in order to achieve proper separation of the whey from the curds.

The milk maturation time is very variable since it depends on the acidity of the milk upon arrival at the cheese factory. In locations where the milking is done very early before the sun gets hot, and where the cheese factory is near the place of milking, it is possible for the milk to arrive very fresh, with 16 or 17 degrees of acidity. In this case, it will be necessary to leave the milk with the lactic culture for at least an hour before curdling, in order for the acidity of the milk to reach 18 or 19 Dornic degrees. In other locations, in spite of early milking, the great distance from the cheese factory means that the milk arrives after two or three hours when its acidity is between 18 and 19 Dornic degrees. The maturation or acidification time of the milk in this case should not exceed half an hour. Finally, it is possible that the milking is done at noon, that is, at the hottest time of day, and the milk reaches the cheese factory at the end of the day after 3 or 4 hours in transit. Under these circumstances it is likely that the milk already has too much acidity and therefore its maturation time should be nil, in other words the rennet should be added immediately after adding the lactic culture to the milk. In fact, it may be necessary to add some water if the acidity is greater than 21 Dornic degrees, since excess acidity as well as the lack of acidity results in imperfections in the cheese.

Coagulation

Coagulation is judged subjectively by the cheesemaker, by carefully examining the coagulum on the vat side, using a finger or probe.

The degree or quality of coagulation determines the final moisture content of the cheese and, since the amount of water present affects the fermentation process and therefore the final texture of the product, coagulation is a crucial step in the cheesemaking process.

The process is based on rennet (or other coagulating enzymes), an enzyme which coagulates milk by bonding the principal protein, casein, into a network which entraps the fat. There are three distinct phases:
1. Casein and calcium (Ca^{2+}) are found in a free state in milk.
2. The enzyme, rennin, attacks the micelles of casein and breaks them down, facilitating the union with calcium.
3. The calcium forms bridges between the micelles of casein to form a smooth, white, gelatinous coagulum incorporating a large part of the fat.

Rennet

The enzyme rennin is found in both natural and substitute rennets. Natural rennet is a substance produced in the stomach walls of calves, lambs and kids and used to coagulate their mothers' milk. Substitute rennets, in tablet, powdered or liquid form are generally processed and purified in commercial laboratories using substances made from moulds, namely mucormieli or mucopusillus. These are similar to pepsin and cymacin, which are the enzymes taken from the stomach of animals to make natural rennet. It can be produced in large quantities, making it cheaper than natural rennet.

Factors affecting the action of rennin

The enzymatic action of rennin is affected by temperature, acidity, salt,

29

light, air, age, and the source and method of preparation:

○ Rennin is very active and coagulation is rapid at high temperatures: 34 to 36°C. Curd formed at this temperature will be firm and can be cut into large pieces (see p.33) suitable for soft cheese. Within limits, the higher the temperature the more moisture will remain and the softer the cheese. Hard cheese, made from small curds requires a relatively low temperature: 31 to 33°C. At lower temperatures, say 20 to 30°C, milk coagulates very slowly and the subsequent curds will be weak with a lot of fat lost to the whey. In any case, the temperature must remain constant: milk that is allowed to cool during the process will produce irregular curds, have unevenly distributed moisture and lose some casein into the whey.

If the milk is either too cold or too hot the rennin will not be active at all.

○ Milk with a high level of acidity will coagulate quickly (and vice versa); this also depends on acidity.

○ Standard preparations of rennet will already contain salt, which would have been added to preserve the rennet.

○ As soon as rennet is exposed to light, air and age it begins to lose strength and, as it weakens, increasingly larger quantities must be used until eventually it ceases to be active altogether. Rennet must be stored in a cool, dry, dark place, measured with clean, dry utensils and handled with clean, dry hands. It should last for a number of months in the refrigerator.

Method of coagulation

Ensure milk is at the appropriate temperature (34 to 36°C for soft cheese; 31 to 33°C for hard cheese). Use 2.5g rennet to 150 litres of milk (or according to instructions). It is normal practice to dilute the liquid rennet (or dissolved powder) with water simply to facilitate mixing a small quantity in a large volume of milk.

Add to the milk. Stir in well for two to five minutes, then leave undisturbed for 30 to 40 minutes. The curd will be ready when it separates easily from the wall of the vat and splits, but does not stick or crack when penetrated with a spoon or finger.

Chapter 2
Curd

Cutting

There are two phases of the cutting of the curd. The first phase consists of inserting the cutting harp into the vat just along its inner edge and beginning to cut the curd in one direction. Each time the opposite end of the vat is reached, a 180 degree turn is made, lifting the harp a bit but not totally removing it from the vat in order not to damage the curd. Upon arriving at the other edge of the vat, the curd is then cut crosswise, that is, at right angles to the previous cutting direction. The same cutting procedure is followed, such that a criss-cross pattern appears in the curd and vertical strips are formed. At this point there is a pause in the cutting and the sectioned curd is left to rest for five minutes, during which time the whey begins to separate from the solids.

Next the second stage of the cutting begins. The vertical strips of curd are turned with the help of plastic plates that are moved by a second worker, and are then cut with the harp which is passed through them in a perpendicular manner. Grains or cubes of curd are formed in this way. The number of passes made depends upon the size of grain desired. In principle, in order to obtain a semi-hard cheese, an attempt is made to cut the curd in grains of 6 to 7mm in diameter. However in practice, the grain size is between 5 and 10mm, a variation that is perhaps due to the difficulty of the operation and the inexperience of the cheesemakers. As a general rule, the grains of curd should have a size similar to a medium-sized kernel of corn.

The entire curd cutting process lasts about 10 or 15 minutes. The cutting of the curd must be done with much care, since if it is not cut correctly there will be many losses due to the pulverization of the grains (grains cut too small) and to the separation of fat, which, upon mixing with the whey, changes the latter from an almost transparent yellow-green to a whitish colour. These problems will reduce the yield of the conversion of milk to cheese.

Photo 1. First crosswise cutting.

Photo 2. Circular cutting.

An easy way to gauge the size of the curds.	
Type of cheese	*Size of curd required*
Fresh	up to 2cm in diameter
Andean (soft)	lima bean (1.5cm)
Tilsit (semi-hard)	maize grain (1cm)
Gruyere (hard)	wheat/rice grain (0.5cm)

Stirring

Stirring, or agitating the curds (Photo 3), separates them from the warm whey and causes them to shrink and increase in density as a result of the whey loss. For hard cheeses, the major part of the whey must be removed from within the grains of curd or the cheese will be too moist and, as excess moisture and excess lactose favour the multiplication of microbes, it will not have a long shelf life.

Stirring should gradually quicken so that grains of curd move swiftly along the surface of the whey. The time required for stirring varies according to the type of cheese being made: curds for soft cheese, which requires large grains with a high moisture content, should not be stirred for long, while those for semi-hard and hard cheeses should be stirred for longer, to produce small grains with a low moisture content.

Increased levels of acidity and temperatures facilitate the

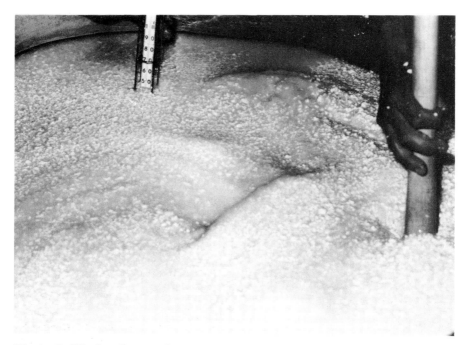

Photo 3. Stirring the curd.

construction of the curd grains. If the milk is very acid, or stirred at too high a temperature, then the curd will be too hard and the stirring will have to be accelerated.

Removal of whey

After stirring has stopped, the grains of curd sink to the bottom of the vat because of their greater density and the whey can be removed. Occasionally, however, curds will float, usually due to the presence of carbon dioxide from coliform contaminations. The whey is skimmed from the vat with a plastic or stainless bucket, changing the position of the bucket so that the mat of curd at the bottom of the vat is not pressed in the same spot. Normally about 30 per cent of whey is removed; more, if acidity is more than 13° Dornic. Whey can be removed from the base of a vat if a suitable drain-lock and sieve are used.

Washing and salting

Washing the curds by adding and stirring warm water enables the removal of the remaining lactose and lactic acid, and adds water. This is suitable only for the washed-curd types of cheese, such as Swiss and

34

Dutch cheeses. The addition of salt during washing helps prevent the growth of microbes and gives the cheese a longer shelf life.

Certain cheeses — Tilsit and Danbo, for example — need hot water (65 to 75°C). In these cases it is very important that the water is added slowly and steadily while the curds are being stirred. This process should take five to ten minutes. If not done correctly, the curds will form hard crusts and retain moisture instead of expelling it.

While the water is being added, the curds must be stirred continually. This stirring continues for a specific period of time, depending on the type of cheese. Very soft cheeses, for example, need only 10 minutes from the moment the water is first added. A semi-hard cheese (Tilsit, Danbo) needs about 30 minutes of stirring in all. A very hard cheese (Gruyère, Parmesan) needs 60 to 80 minutes. During this process, the whey is expelled from the curds. Most of the whey is then removed with plastic dippers to facilitate gathering the curds for the subsequent moulding.

Moulding and Pressing

To shape the cheeses, the curds are packed into moulds. The moulding table is covered with a thick nylon mesh (2 mm squares). The moulds are placed on top of this mesh so that the cheeses may acquire a pleasing grid pattern on the outside. While one person stirs the curds, another scoops them out and pours them into the moulds, until they are full (Photos 4 and 5). The whey drains out through the holes in the sides of the moulds and base. Drainage can be speeded up by lightly pressing down on the curds with the hands. In about five minutes, all the visible whey will have been drained and a compact mass will have formed. The cheeses are then ready to be turned over for the first time. The subsequent pressing process depends on the type of cheese.

Soft cheeses, made from large curds, are not pressed because they would lose too much humidity. After the curds have been placed in the moulds, their own weight provides sufficient pressure to form the cheeses. The correct room temperature is absolutely essential for this process: it must be warm, with 20°C being the optimal temperature to allow the specific bacteria to grow and produce the correct acidity. This acidity in turn allows the whey to drain off, without any extra pressure. To maintain the 20°C temperature, the doors of the moulding room must be kept closed. The run-off beneath the moulds should be rinsed away with the warm whey (never with cold water) to avoid an abrupt drop in temperature. In high altitudes and colder climates, the moulding cheeses must be covered with a large piece of plastic to keep them at 20°C.

Hard and semi-hard cheeses, made from small- and medium-sized

35

Photo 4. Moulding the Andean cheese (Nabuzo communal cheese factory).

Photo 5. Moulding the South American white cheese in plastic moulds 10cm in diameter, 25cm in height and with perforations of 3mm.

curds, are pressed for specific lengths of time depending on the type of cheese. Each cheese in its mould is wrapped in a cloth, with the edges folded up smoothly over the top. A piece of wood, shaped to fit into the mould, is placed on top of the cloth. A round piece of cement, made to fit into the mould, is placed on top of the wood. Generally, 4kg of weight are needed for Andean cheese, 6kg for Tilsit, and 10 for Danbo. Danbo cheese is made in a rectangular mould with rectangular weights.

The cheeses are removed from the moulds after a half an hour. The cloths are wrung out to remove the whey and any dry crusts that have formed around the edges of the cheeses are cut off. The cheeses are turned upside down and placed back into the moulds. They are then rewrapped (called 'dressing') in the cloth and weighed down again for another hour, then unwrapped, unmoulded, and turned over again. Next, the cheeses are returned to the moulds and placed on a dry cloth, unwrapped. They are left sitting until the next day (approximately 12 to 14 hours). During this entire process, an effort must be made to keep the room temperature as close to 20°C as possible. An experienced cheesemaker will, at this point, have a good idea how successful the fermentation process has been. The cheese should be yellow, with a firm texture, and the top edges should have pulled away slightly from the mould. A poorly processed cheese will be pale, with a mounded top and its edges touching the mould all the way around. This can result from the presence of coliforms or any gas-producing micro-organism; even reactivation of the starter culture can cause gas formation. These cheeses will swell to form bloated balls and the only way to save them is to process them immediately into Mozzarella or Provolone (see p.44). It is very important for the cheesemaker to realize that coliform gassy fermentation is a serious problem and s/he must recheck the entire process used, including milk quality, culture and general hygiene procedures.

The moulding of Gruyère cheese is a difficult operation. A thin steel strip is fitted on the edge of a coarse-woven dipping cloth, overlapping slightly. The steel-edged cloth is passed down and under the curd bed in one smooth swoop. The four corners of the dipping cloth are brought together to form a bag, and the filled bag of curd is pulled out of the whey, then deposited directly into a round, wooden Gruyère cheese hoop. Remove the small amount of curd left in the bottom of the vat and quickly return it to the curd bed. Fold over the heavy cloth and knead the cheese lightly with the palms of the hands.

A Gruyère cheese, which is very large, needs a great deal of pressure — about 10 times its own weight. The pressing should be gradual: a little pressure at first, then slowly increase the weight. If the pressure is too heavy at the beginning, while the cheese still has a lot of whey, a thick crust will form around the entire cheese, preventing the rest of the whey from draining out. The end result will be a cheese with a hard, dry outer layer and a white spongy acidic inner layer, with drops of whey. As it continues to mature, the flavour will become bitter.

To facilitate whey separation from curd:
○ The temperature should be 31° to 33°C
○ Add more rennet to reduce coagulation time
○ Prevent too rapid acidification, avoid milk that is overripe or too much culture
○ Cut the curd earlier
○ Cut the curd into finer (rice-sized) grains
○ Increase stirring to two hours
○ Increase temperature during stirring to 55°C (for Parmesan)
○ Turn the cheese more frequently in the moulds.

To slow down the whey separation from curd:
○ Use pasteurized milk
○ Raise temperatures for coagulation (35°C in Andean or lower in Camembert, 26 to 29°C)
○ Cut the curd after it has become well stiffened
○ Cut the grains larger
○ Stir slowly for a shorter time
○ Increase the temperature of the hot water used during the second stirring to form a hard surface that will prevent the escape of whey
○ Salt the curd.

Weighing

After 24 hours remove the cheese from the mould, weigh it to calculate the conversion from milk into cheese and identify each cheese clearly with the date of its pressing.

Conversion

The conversion or yield from milk to cheese varies considerably, but depends to a large degree on the fat and protein content of the milk, the quantity of fat lost during cheesemaking and the amount of water absorbed during the stiffening process (see Figure 12 and Table). Other factors also play a part; in Europe, for example, the yield from autumn milk is higher than from spring milk due to the higher protein content of the former and its mineral balance (see also p.14). A high conversion cheese — one which requires less milk for the same quantity of cheese — will be cheaper to produce and more cost-effective than a low conversion cheese. Conversion may be expressed either as the quantity of milk required to produce 1kg of cheese or by the number of kilograms of cheese obtained from 100 litres of milk:

Yield of cheese from milk.

	No. of litres of milk required for 1kg cheese	No. of kg of cheese produced from 100 litres milk
Fresh cheese	7.5	13.3
Andean cheese	8.5	11.8
Tilsit	9.5	10.5
Danbo	9.5	10.5
Gruyère	11	9.1
Provolone	11.5	8.7
Parmesan	12	8.3
Mozzarella (fresh Provolone)	10.5	9.5

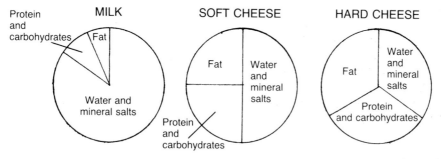

Figure 12. Relative composition of milk and cheese.

Relative composition of milk, soft cheese and hard cheese.

	Milk	Soft cheese	Hard cheese
Fats	40g	240g	315g
Protein	35g	205g	275g
Carbohydrate	48g	25g	25g
Mineral Salts	7g	20g	25g
Water	870g	500g	350g
Salt		10g	10g
Vitamins	ABDEK	ABDEK	ABDEK

Brining

Brine, a known solution of salt in water, forms the cheese rind. The salt solution hardens the outer layer of the cheese by drawing off the moisture from the surface of the cheese. The final texture of the rind depends on the salinity, acidity and temperature of the brine: too little salt will not draw off enough moisture and the rind will not be properly hardened. Too much acidity will damage both the rind and the cheese during ageing, and if the brine is too cold then there will be insufficient exchange of whey and salt and the rind will be soft.

Method

Boil 30 litres of water and, while it is still hot, dissolve in it 10kg of salt. This gives a salinity of about 20 to 22°C Baumé. Cool the brine to 12°C before submerging the cheese. Salt may be sprinkled on the upper side of the cheese to obtain uniformity.

Cheese is left in the brine (Photo 6) according to its size, for example: Andean cheese (1.2kg) requires 6 to 8 hours, Tilsit (3kg) 20 to 24 hours and large Gruyère (40kg) 48 hours.

The salinity of the brine gradually decreases and its acidity increases. When the acidity rises above 40°D the brine should be discarded. When the salinity falls below 18° Baumé, salt should be added until it reaches its original salinity. The temperature of the brine must also be checked from time to time and should vary between 8 and 12°C. After brining, remove the cheese, allow it to dry a little and place it on the lower shelves in the maturing room so that it does not drip on to older cheeses.

Photo 6. Tile-covered concrete brining tank (Nabuzo communal cheese plant).

40

Chapter 3
Cheese

Maturation

Maturation, also known as ripening or curing, results in some instances from the growth and multiplication of aerobic microbes on the rind, progressing inward after a few weeks, and produces a well-ripened cheese with a pleasant aroma, flavour and texture. Enzymes, produced by *B. Linens* bacteria in particular, pass into the cheese mass, contributing to the ageing process, and are especially important in the formation of taste and aroma. Not all cheeses rely on microbes entering from the rind — the starter culture microbes or their enzymes will be present throughout the cheese.

Changes in cheese during ripening

Growth of bacteria. Rapid growth takes place during the first few days of the ripening period. One or two grams of three-day-old cheese may contain several hundred million bacteria.

Change in the types of bacteria. During the first few days the streptococcus organisms, chiefly from the starter, are in the majority. Later, lactobacilli and others, like propionic bacteria (in Swiss cheese), predominate. (See Figure 13).

Decrease in sugar content. The remaining lactose present usually disappears in the cheese within a few days.

Decrease in moisture. There is a slow decrease in the percentage of moisture, even in paraffined cheese.

Decrease in acidity. There is a decrease in total acidity as the ripening progresses.

Change in pH. The pH is lowest (most acid) in the cheese about the third or fourth day after moulding. It then increases slowly during the ripening period. A pH level of 5 to 5.2 of cheese after pressing will rise to

41

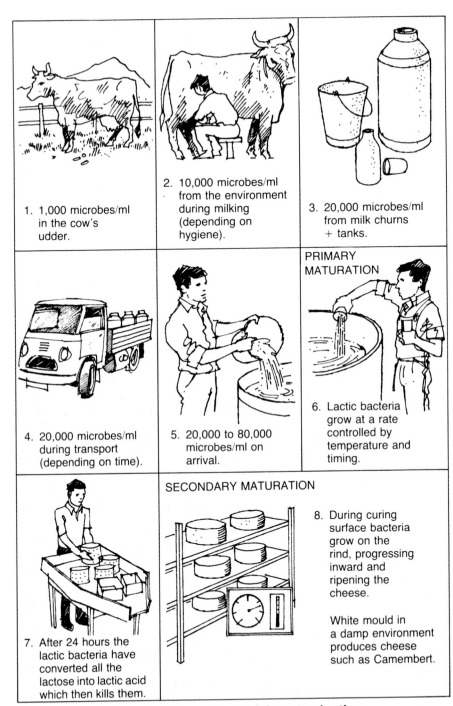

Figure 13. Normal bacterial contamination.

5.4 to 6 after four weeks and 5.8 to 6 after eight weeks. If, however, the pH level drops, the cheese will have a sour or bitter flavour.

Change in the flavour. Good quality cheese kept at 15°C should develop a pleasant, full flavour in four to eight weeks. Certain volatile flavouring compounds are formed.

Change in the body of the cheese. The chemical and physical properties of the casein change as the ripening progresses. Increasing amounts of casein are changed to a more soluble form by the action of bacteria and enzymes. The change is accelerated at higher ripening temperatures. The body of a good cheese changes from a tough corky-like texture to a smooth, waxy consistency. In acid cheese a mealy, pasty body results.

Production of gas. Gas production is normal in some cheese. It is, of course, abundant if the cheese contains the typical gas-producing bacteria, as with Swiss cheeses.

Conditions

The temperature, relative humidity and ventilation in the maturing rooms where the cheeses remain until their sale all affect the maturation of the cheese. Ideally, the room should be ventilated, but the air should have a relative humidity of about 80 to 90 per cent and the temperature should be between 13 and 15°C. If too low a temperature is used, the cheeses will mature very slowly and may have an acid flavour and a crumbly texture; if too warm, the cheeses will become soft and break down. If the humidity is too low the cheeses dry out, become very hard and will crack; too high and they may become covered with a foul-smelling yellow-white scum. A thermo-hygrometer measures both temperature and relative humidity accurately, but it is sufficient to measure only the temperature daily. The approximate relative humidity can be estimated by inspecting the cheeses, an ability that comes with experience. Dry, cracked cheese indicates a low humidity and yellow surface scum indicates high humidity.

Temperature and humidity can be manipulated in various ways. The room temperature can be raised by opening the door to the production room where the vat is being heated and can be cooled by adding a ceiling or a second roof to prevent direct sunlight or by opening windows at night. Cover the window opening with a fine mesh to prevent insects and other pests from entering. A dry curing room can be made more humid by spraying the walls and floor with water daily, taking care not to wet the cheeses, and by keeping doors and vents closed to prevent the escape of moist air. A more expensive solution is to add pools of water or pipes which wet the walls when necessary. Opening windows and doors might dry out a damp curing room, but in very damp climates it is sometimes necessary to put in moisture-absorbing substances such as sawdust or sand.

Wiping

As the cheese is initially very acid, the lactose having been transformed into lactic acid, bacteria will preferentially grow on the rind. A cheese left unattended in the maturing room will soon become covered with a layer of mould and decay. Wiping the cheeses gently with a moist cloth not only reduces mould formation but can also inoculate a new rind with bacteria from old rind, thereby helping the rind to develop and encouraging the maturation from the surface to the inside of the mass. Smearing a liquid bacterial culture on the surface also protects against mould.

Wiping is done in two stages:

1. Wipe the sides and upper face of the cheese with a moist cloth, keeping the shelf dry.

2. Two days later turn the cheese over and wipe the other face and the sides.

Provolone

Smoked Provolone

Smoked Provolone belongs to the 'pasta filata' or stretched curd category of cheeses traditionally produced in Italy, Bulgaria, Rumania and Turkey. It is related to Caciocavallo and Mozzarella. It is made from fresh milk, raw or pasteurized, though slightly sour milk can be used. Bacterial starters are added to achieve a specific level of acidity and curds are formed by the coagulating action of rennet. Andean cheese, Tilsit and Danbo are all made in a similar way. However, for Provolone, instead of moulding, the curds are piled onto a table and left to ferment. After fermentation, the curds are cut and heated in water and then stretched and rolled into round, pear-like or sausage shapes. The weight can vary from 450 to 2,270g. The cheeses are hung in plastic or string nets during the subsequent drying and ripening. The outside has a shiny surface, smooth and well-sealed, without cracks or holes. After hanging the cheese turns yellow and is then ready to be smoked, if required, which imparts the characteristic pleasant smokey aroma of this popular cheese.

Raw material and acidity test

Smoked Provolone is made from curd which has fermented over a 15- to 30-hour period at 20°C. The acidity of the curd is the decisive factor in forming smooth and well-shaped cheeses. In hot weather, 15 hours of fermentation is enough, whereas in cooler periods, up to 30 hours are needed.

A simple test after fermentation determines the correct acidity and therefore the right moment to begin stretching and moulding: take a one cm strip of curd and submerge it in water (65°C) for two minutes. Remove it and stretch it. If it stretches smoothly to approximately double its length, it is ready. If not, or if it breaks, it needs to ferment longer to increase the acidity. If the curds are not acid enough the curd will be lumpy. On the other hand, if the curd stretches very quickly and is very soft it has overfermented and the strings will break and not hold together during shaping.

In rural cheese factories, Provolone has been successfully produced from curds which had been intended for Danbo/Tilsit or Andean cheese, but which had suffered from coliform gas fermentation and were therefore disqualified from the ripening process. These cheeses have to be processed within a maximum of 40 hours after moulding.

Hot-water processing

When the curds are ready to be stretched, cut them with a large knife into narrow strips, not more than one cm wide.

Heat a large (50 litre) pan with 20 litres of water to 80°C. Add about 20kg of the strips of curd to the water, making sure that all the curd is covered by water. Leave the curds submerged for 5 to 10 minutes, allowing the water temperature to drop to 65°C. Using a large wooden paddle, begin stretching the curds with a pulling movement. Continue until a smooth, uniform, white plastic mass forms. At this point, place the paddle under the curds and lift them out, letting the mass fall on either side of the paddle. Pull out a segment of the mass with both hands, pulling, stretching and squeezing it, and smoothing out holes, lumps, rough parts, drops of water or whey (Photos 7 and 8). Then let it fall back into the water and begin again with another segment. If the curds have not been well worked, they retain a great deal of whey, which is discarded during the ripening process, leaving folds in the surface of the cheese.

During this entire process, the temperature of the water and the curds must remain at between 60 and 65°C.

Moulding

When the mass of curd is shiny and of a uniform consistency, pull a

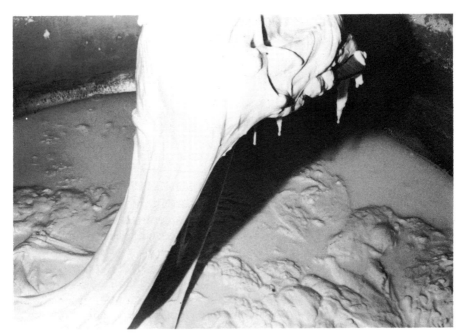

Photo 7. During hot-water processing a uniform, plastic mass forms.

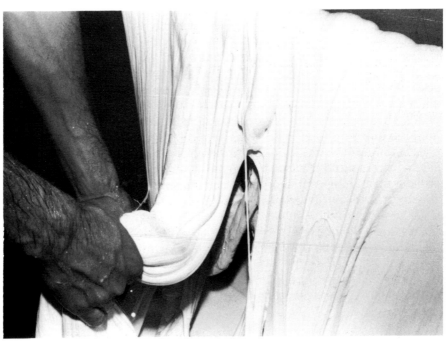

Photo 8. Holes, lumps and drops of whey are squeezed out with the hands.

46

segment and begin to roll the curds up into a very tight shape, rotating the ball until it reaches the desired size. This must be done by pulling firmly and steadily on the curds so that each thin layer will join the one beneath. If this is not done properly, air pockets and whey will be trapped between the layers of the cheese and create an imperfect product. When fully formed, the hot ball of cheese is placed in the middle of a piece of thin cloth, 50cm square. The cloth is folded lengthwise over the cheese and its ends are twisted in opposite directions, compressing the cheese and removing the last drops of whey.

Cooling and brine solution

The cheese is removed from the cloth and tossed into a cold water-bath to cool. The bath must be kept constantly cold by a flow of running water. After approximately two to four hours the cheeses are removed from the cold water-bath and placed in a brine solution (20 to 22° Baumé) for four to six hours, according to their size. The brine solution is prepared by adding 10kg of industrial salt to 30 litres of boiled water. Since the cheeses float, extra salt must be sprinkled on top to obtain uniform salinity.

Drying and weighing

After the salt bath, the cheeses are placed in a net bag made from either plastic or string. They are tied together in pairs and hung over a stick for three to five days to dry (Photo 9). Once dry, all the cheeses from the same batch are weighed together to determine the yield produced from the fresh milk.

Smoking

Smoking gives the cheese its characteristic golden colour and appealing aroma and flavour. It also acts as a germicide on the surface of the cheese. It is important that the smoke does not heat the cheese directly. An effective design, therefore, is to produce the smoke away from the smoking room, so that only the cool smoke reaches the cheeses (Photo 10). When the fire is burning well, sawdust is added to produce copious amounts of smoke. Smoking takes four to eight hours, depending on the intensity of the smoke, until the cheeses are shiny and golden coloured. Care must be taken to select wood from a safe source; industrial cuts are unsuitable, for instance.

Yield

The yield of Provolone cheese is less than other types of cheese, since part of the milk fat is not incorporated into the curds, but is lost in the

Photo 9. The cheeses are hung in net bags to dry.

Photo 10. A suitable smoking room, with smoke channelled in from outside.

water bath. Ten and a half to eleven litres of milk are needed to obtain 1kg of Provolone cheese.

The smoking process further reduces the weight of the cheese by 10 per cent. If this yield is not obtained, too much milk fat has been lost in the water bath, either because of low acidification of the curds or overlong submersion in the hot-water bath.

Ripening and preservation

Smoked Provolone cheese can be consumed immediately after smoking, when the smoky flavour is most prominent. It can also be preserved for several weeks, which hardens and ripens the cheese. The ideal conditions for ripening consist of a 14 to 16°C temperature and an 80 per cent humidity. However, in the tropics, Provolone has been successfully ripened at 20°C and 95 per cent humidity.

Undesirable bacterial growth seldom presents problems during the ripening process, due to the high acidification and temperature of the curds during stretching. This process destroys the majority of micro-organisms and inhibits the development of surviving bacteria.

The main problems are external, such as fly larvae on the surface of the cheese. Ants and cockroaches have also been known to descend the strips. Moulds can grow, too, when there is excessive humidity. In this case, the cheeses must be cleaned with a dry cloth.

To avoid these problems, and to conserve the moisture in the cheese, the cheeses can be wiped with vegetable oil or with a plastic solution (Mowilith or Foodplast) which also improves their external appearance. As the cheese ripens, the acidic taste is replaced by a sharp, highly aromatic flavour and the texture becomes firmer and drier. Occasionally 'eyes' will appear in the body of the cheese, due to gaseous fermentations.

Use of the by-products

The whey or water mixture left after the stretching of the cheese is rich in fat. It can be passed through a cream separator, or just left to set overnight and the resulting fat can be skimmed off and made into butter.

Disadvantages of Provolone cheese

○ The processing is slightly difficult at first, until one becomes accustomed to judging the correct moment to begin the stretching and pulling.
○ The temperature of the curds is quite high and takes getting used to.
○ The yield is low, which causes the price of the cheese to be higher than other cheeses.

49

Mozzarella cheese

Mozzarella is a soft, white cheese, similar to Provolone, but with a higher whey content and is sold fresh. It is packed in plastic bags and needs to be refrigerated for not more than about 10 days. Consumers prefer low-fat Mozzarella (30 per cent fat) for dietetic purposes. It is often used as a pizza topping, since it forms the characteristic long strands when heated.

The production of Mozzarella is the same as that for Provolone until the curds are about to be stretched. Then they are worked only half as long as the time taken for the Provolone curds, leaving more whey in the curds. They are stretched and rolled into firm balls, as with Provolone, but instead of being squeezed in the cloths and put into cold water they are immediately put into plastic bags and sealed. They are put next to one another on shelves, in a cold room (4°C), to be delivered as soon as they are cool, (normally the next day). Mozzarella can also be dried in a cold room without the plastic bags, producing a firm texture which is easier to slice, often preferred by Pizzerias.

The yield of wet Mozzarella is 1kg per 10.5 litres of milk with three per cent butterfat.

Preserving and record keeping

Preserving cheese

A well-made cheese will last for a long time. Nevertheless, some factories add sodium or potassium nitrate to the milk to prevent the swelling up of the cheese caused by coli or butyric bacteria. These additives are not always successful however: active aerobic coli bacteria in milk, for example, prevent potassium nitrate from working and can produce a bitter taste in the cheese, lowering its quality. It is better to eliminate the need for preservatives by ensuring that good hygiene prevails at all times.

Record keeping

A record (see Figure 14) of daily procedures can help analyse and understood successful and unsuccessful batches. The record should include all the items given in the box.

Common problems and their causes

Cheese with cracks

Over-acidified milk or carelessness with starters and production can result in too much whey remaining in the cheese. During secondary maturation, the necessary enzymes will be unable to penetrate the cheese from the rind to the centre, often producing a cheese with two

Daily technical report

1. date	13. amount of salt added
2. quantity of milk in vat	14. time in minutes for washing and
3. type of cheese to be made	stirring
4. quantity of fat in the milk	15. temperature of whey after final
5. acid level of milk	watering
6. type and quantity of culture and	16. total time of preparation from
amount of rennet used	rennet to pressing
7. temperature of coagulation	17. number of moulds
8. time in minutes of cutting and	18. weight of new cheese before
stirring	brine bath
9. size of curds	19. weight of cheese after maturation
10. acidity of whey	20. conversion of milk to cheese
11. amount of whey extracted	21. observations
12. amount of water added	

colours, which is ripe on the outside but bitter and crumbly within. Specific causes can be one or more of the following:

○ Undue care at milking
○ Milk exposed to sunlight (that is, heat) resulting in high acidity
○ Dirty milk churns
○ Negligence and delays in manufacture

Early blow-ups (Pressler defect)

Blow-ups, where the cheese becomes full of small or large bubbles of gas, can occur during pressing (called the Pressler defect). They are normally caused by *Aerobacter aerogenes* or *Escherichia coli* entering the milk during milking or transport or through cloths or cloth filters and are invariably due to a lack of hygiene, such as:

○ Unhygienic milking or dirty cloths
○ Dirty churns
○ Milk containing antibiotics or other inhibiting substances (mastitis, for example) which sets back growth of the desired bacteria.
○ Degenerated cultures
○ Dirty water
○ Unhygienic workers.

Blow-ups can be prevented if the level of milk contamination is slight with an active culture of streptococcus, but nothing can prevent the growth of coliforms if milk is contaminated by antibiotics.

Late blow-ups

Clostridia are mobile, anaerobic and spore-forming microbes. They are present in large quantities in faeces and produce large quantities of carbon dioxide and hydrogen gas and cannot be eliminated by

51

No.	PRODUCER	Den. 1	Temp. 2	Corr 3	Fat 4	N.F.S 5	Red. 6	FERMENTATION
1	Esperanza Chávez	29	25	31	3.3%	8.67	5	gelatinous I
2	Galuth Chamorro	29	23	30.6	4.1	8.73	7	"
3	Juan Chamorro	29	24	30.8	4.3	8.82	4	"
4	Rosa Masabanda	27½	26	29.7	4.1	8.50	3	"
5	Gonzalo Chamorro	29.5	29	32.3	3.6	9.05	6.30	spongy II
6	Maria Chamorro	28	28	30.6	3.2	8.55	6	gelatinous I
7	Arturo Espinoza	28	24	29.8			6	"
8	Edgar Véscones	29	25	31	3.9	8.79	5	gassy III
9	Antonio Vargas	31.5	23	33.3	2.8	9.14	6	gelatinous I
10	Muscline Castro	29.5	25	31.5	2.9	8.71	5	spongy II
11	Aurelio López	28.5	26	30.7	3.4	8.61	5.30	"
12	Rodrigo Vargas	28.5	25	30.5	3.5	8.58	4.30	"
13	Gladis Salazar	29.5	27	31.9	2.4	8.81	6.30	gelatinous I
14	Pedro Vega	29	25	31	3.1	8.63	7	"
15	Nicanor López	29	24	30.8	3.2	8.65	5	spongy I
16	Betty Chamorro	28.5	25	30.5	3.5	8.58	5	gelatinous I
17	Rosa Valle	26	28	28.6	3.8	8.17	4	"
18	Marcelino Yáswnez	28.5	22	29.9	4.1	8.55	6	"
19	Luis Chamorro	27.5	25	29.5	4.3	8.49	6	spongy & gassy
20	Anita Collay	28	27	30.8	3.3	8.72	4.30	spongy I
21	Julio Cadena	29	23	30.6	4.8	8.87	7	gelatinous I
22	Paila	28	28	30.6	3.5	8.61	3	spongy II

```
1. Density
2. Temperature
3. Correction
4. Fat
5. Non-fat solids
6. Reductase
```

Laboratory Manager   Plant Manager

Salinas, a 22 de Abril 1988

▨▨▨▨ Results exceeding established limits of factory

Figure 14. Example of record keeping.

52

1. Unhygienic milking
   near manure and muck

2. Rotten silage for feed

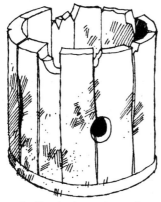

3. Cracked wooden pails

Blow ups occur after
several weeks, when the pH
level reaches 6.5-6.8
— the optimum pH level
for *Clostridium
tyrobutyricum*

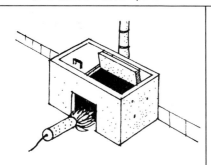

4. Pasteurization
   cannot eliminate
   clostridia

5. There is no remedy

Figure 15. Late blow ups.

pasteurization. These bacteria enter the milk from the hands or clothing of personnel or when tiny bits of excrement fall into churns and milking equipment. Care must be taken to avoid, in particular:

○ Unhygienic milking near manure and muck
○ Rotten silage for feed.

The only defence is to prevent the bacteria entering the milk and the importance of good hygiene cannot be overemphasized.

Photos 11 and 12. Cheeses in Ecuador: imaginative packaging is very important.

Part III
Beyond cheesemaking

Chapter 1
Other foods from milk

Whey

The whey removed from the cheese vat after the initial stirring of the curd and before the addition of hot water and salt is rich in fat and albumin, a milk protein which is not coagulated by rennet.

The appropriate composition of whey is:

water	93%
lactose	4.8%
protein (albumin)	0.7%
fat	0.8%
minerals	0.7%

The mineral salts and lactose, the major solid component creating the sweet flavour of the whey, are dissolved in the whey and can only be recovered by the concentration of the whey by evaporation to 60 per cent solids followed by cooling. The fat can be removed either with a mechanical decreamer, or by leaving the whey overnight until the cream rises to the surface. This cream makes a butter which is considered to have an inferior taste but which is excellent for baking. The albumin can be separated from acidified whey and used with or without fat to make Ricotta. After the fat and protein have been removed, the whey, which is rich in lactose and mineral salts, is usually fed to farm animals (Figure 16).

Ricotta (whey cheese)

Fresh Ricotta has a bland flavour and is made from albumin, obtained by heating whole or separated acidified whey, to which milk may have been added.

Method

Preparing the bacterial culture

Incubate a few bottles of whey from the cheese vat at 38°C for 24 hours

55

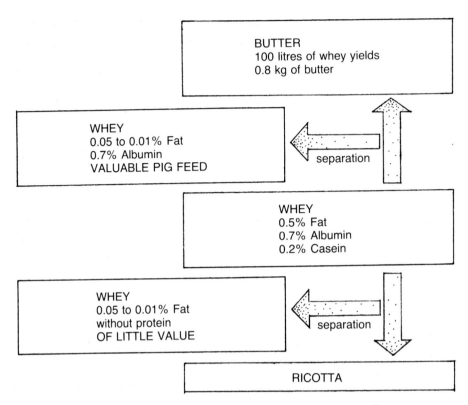

Figure 16. Transformation of whey and its by-products.

until it reaches an acid level of 200° Dornic. A small quantity of yoghurt starter culture may be added to stimulate acidification.

Heating the whey

Heat the whey to 80 to 85°C. It should not be acidified until it reaches the indicated temperature. Add about 10 per cent of the whey starter, or 250g of granular citric acid dissolved in two litres of water for 500 litres of whey, or 0.4 per cent white vinegar. Stop the agitation after the addition. Continued heating carries the submerged curd particles to the surface, but the fire should be kept very low. Let the curd rest for 15 minutes. Floating is influenced by the amount of fat and acid. Adding some skimmed milk or buttermilk, when the whey reaches 85°C helps to trap fine particles of albumin more effectively by collecting them into larger units. Buttermilk gives the product a smoother and softer texture. If too much agitation is applied or there is excess acid, the curd mass will settle to the bottom of the vat and the separation from the whey will be very difficult.

Transfer the floating curd from the surface into a fine cheesecloth with a perforated scoop. If the precipitated albumin fails to rise to the surface, the whey may be strained through fine cheesecloth into another tank. Tie the four corners of the cheesecloth together and suspend it above the draining tank for four to six hours to drain.

It is difficult to believe that acid cheese, which has been sterilized at more than 80°C is so susceptible to microbial spoilage. Ricotta cannot be preserved for very long because of its high moisture content, and should be eaten fresh, either on its own, or with salt, spices, sugar cinnamon or with sweet fritters.

Conversion

One hundred litres of whole whey contains approximately 700 grams of albumin and 800 grams of fat — a total of 1.5kg of removable solids. This yields 3kg of Ricotta, since Ricotta contains more than 50 per cent of water. Given this low yield, the cheapest form of fuel available should be used.

Cream

Cream, the concentrated fat from milk, is derived directly either from milk or from the whey.

The cream from milk differs in composition from the cream obtained from whey, and the composition can be measured with a butyrometer or simply by eye.

The composition of cream.

	Milk cream	Whey cream
water	60.0%	58.0%
fat	35.0%	37.0%
lactose	2.5%	3.5%
protein	2.0%	1.0%
minerals	5%	0.5%

Milk fat has a relative density of 0.93, less than water (1,000 litres of milk weigh 1,031kg, while 1,000 litres of cream weigh 930kg); consequently, as cream is less dense than milk, the cream rises to the surface of the milk.

Separating, or skimming the milk or whey, is the first step in buttermaking and can be done in two ways: naturally or mechanically.

Natural separation

The milk is left to stand undisturbed overnight so that the cream rises to the surface and can be skimmed off with a spatula or flat spoon, agitating the milk as little as possible. This traditional way of removing cream, used by cheesemakers who have no machinery, has the disadvantage of leaving a relatively large amount (more than one per cent) of cream in the milk.

Mechanical separation

Milk passes through a high velocity centrifuge (Figure 17). This separates the milk from the cream and they each flow out of separate outlets. Mechanical separation is more expensive, but is more rapid and efficient than natural decreaming. The cream is almost completely separated from the milk, which contains only 0.05 to 0.10 per cent fat. Large decreaming machines have a dial which controls the percentage of cream to be removed.

Pasteurization of cream

Fresh cream contains large numbers of bacteria which will damage butter and therefore should be pasteurized to eliminate all bacteria, both harmful and beneficial. As cream is more viscous than milk, it requires a

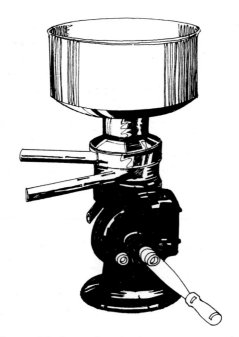

Figure 17. A mechanical cream separator.

58

slightly more severe pasteurization: it should be heated to 75°C for 10 to 20 minutes.

Butter

Whey cream butter, having passed through the long cheesemaking process, has a shorter shelf-life than milk cream butter. Special attention should, therefore, be paid to maintain the correct pasteurization temperatures.

Maturation

For cultured butter cool the cream to 25°C after pasteurization, a favourable temperature for the development of the bacteria in lactic starters. Add five per cent lactic culture, with flavour-producing bacteria, and leave the cream for 10 to 16 hours, until it develops an acid taste. If left for too long, the cream will become so acidified that whey will begin to appear at the bottom of the tank; this is not desirable. As a general rule, the cream should not exceed 45 to 55° Dornic. Cool the cream to 12°C.

Churning

Churning — throwing the cream against a surface — transforms it into butter. The cream thickens and becomes spongy as the fat globules mass together, becoming solid grain-size pieces of butter which float to the surface of the cream whey, the whitish liquid called buttermilk. As soon as the cream thickens and before the grains of butter form a mass, the churning should stop. Either the whey should be drained off or the butter strained out with a sieve. If the grains of butter are allowed to stick together they will re-absorb droplets of whey, increasing the amount of lactose present and giving the butter a short shelf-life. Churning normally takes 20 to 40 minutes and a churning temperature of 12 to 14°C should be observed.

Washing

Washing the butter grains prolongs its shelf life by removing any residue whey. Excessive washing, however, can destroy its taste and aroma. The water — spring- or rain-water is suitable — must be clean and free from harmful bacteria, or the effects of pasteurization will be annulled. The water should also be cool — between 10 and 12°C — in fact, the cooler the better.

Washing three times is usually sufficient to remove the buttermilk residue: when the rinse water running off the butter is clear rather than cloudy, the butter is ready.

Salting

Salt is added to butter to improve its flavour and help to preserve it, as salt delays the growth of microbes. There are two methods for salting butter:

○ *Dry salting.* Here, two to three per cent of fine clean salt is added to the butter after washing and carefully mixed in to ensure uniformity.

○ *Wet salting.* This method is used when fine salt is not available. Between two and three per cent of clean coarse salt is added to the final washing water. It must be well-dissolved and if not completely *clean* or dissolved the solution should be filtered several times before use. The butter should not be allowed to mass together before the salt solution is added or the butter will not be evenly salted.

Pressing

Pressing the butter, either manually or mechanically, removes any droplets of water that remain from washing in order to further its shelf life.

Butter churns usually have a pair of rollers which press the butter after washing is complete.

Moulding and packing

Butter is moulded into small blocks of one quarter or half a kilo with wooden forms and tops. These forms must be moist and cool so that the butter does not stick. After moulding the forms are often lined with wax paper that adheres to the butter when they are removed. The butter is packed in opaque cartons to ensure that light, which rapidly turns butter rancid, does not penetrate.

Composition

Good butter should have an adequate fat and a low moisture content — less than 16 per cent. It should not contain much protein nor lactose as these components would feed unwanted bacteria. Unsalted butter must be especially well-treated in order to keep an agreeable taste and aroma.

Butter is composed of:

Fat	81%
Water	16%
Salt	2.5%
Protein	0.5%

1. Pasteurize the milk for 30 minutes at 80 to 85°C.

2. Sterilize the yoghurt jars in boiling water for 15 minutes.

3. Cool the milk to 45°C.

4. Add 1 teaspoon of live yoghurt per litre of milk and mix well.

5. Pour the milk into the sterilized jars and cover to avoid contamination.

6. Put the jars in warm water (35 to 42°C). The water should not cool below 35°C.

7. After four or five hours the yoghurt is ready. Remove the jars and keep them cool.

Yoghurt contains the bacteria *Streptococcus Thermophilus* and *Lactobacillus Bulgaricus* which are beneficial to human digestion. Yoghurt can be eaten cold, on its own, or mixed with honey, fruit cereal and many other foods.

Special dry cultures are available for industrial yoghurt production but for home-made yoghurt any good natural shop-bought yoghurt may be used as a starter.

Figure 18. Making yoghurt.

61

Conversion tables for cream and butter.

Starting material	Converted material	Yield
Milk 100 litres, 3.3% fat[1]	*Cream* 10 litres, 32% fat	10%
Milk cream 10 litres, 32% fat	*Butter* 4kg, 80% fat	40%
Milk 100 litres	*Butter* 4kg	4%
Whey/Cream/Butter		
Whey 100 litres, 0.5 to 1% fat[2]	*Cream* 1.5 to 3 litres, 33% fat	2%
Whey cream 1.5 to 3 litres	*Butter* 800 to 1,200g	40%

1. If milk is skimmed, 0.1% fat is lost.
2. Buttermilk (0.5 to 1 per cent fat) mixed with cheese whey and passed through a decreamer can yield more cream.

Chapter 2
The rural cheese factory

Location

The location of pasture grounds (so that the milk is not transported too far), climate (temperature and humidity), access to water and drainage are the most essential factors which must be considered when deciding where to build a cheese factory.

In tropical regions cheese factories are usually located at an altitude of 2,000 to 4,000m, where temperatures are ideal for cheese ripening and buttermaking. Rapid temperature changes must be avoided and draughts must be excluded from the factory as much as possible.

As a cheese factory requires large quantities of cool, fresh, bacteria-free water (10 litres for every litre of milk processed — 3,000 litres daily for 300 litres of milk), it should be built, ideally, near a spring or fresh mountain stream and the water piped directly into the plant.

The site should be built above, not below, a town and at least 100m from byres, stables and pig-styes, to avoid contamination from sewers, refuse and animal dirt, and should be elevated to allow fast, easy drainage. People tending animals should not enter the cheese factory.

Construction

Floors

Concrete floors are preferable as they can be washed and drained daily and are strong enough to withstand blows from steel churns and tanks. They should be inclined for fast efficient drainage and must be smooth and unbroken: holes and cracks are difficult to clean and also trap dirt and micro-organisms.

Drainage

Waste water must be carried well away from the plant in closed pipes which are covered at each end with wire screen to exclude rodents and with U bends or other traps to prevent odours entering the factory.

Walls

Cement walls should be painted with lime to kill microbes and repainted every three months. A sandy plaster applied to a height of one metre allows the walls to be hosed down. If available, tiles make an excellent surface in the cheese room and plastic or rubberized paints are useful, if available.

Roof

Tile roofing is a good insulator, keeping out excessive heat or cold. If galvanized roofing is used, insulated ceilings must be installed as well, to prevent fluctuations of temperature. A small roofed lintel over the main door helps to prevent an accumulation of muck on the entrance floor. Beware: condensation on the underside of galvanized roofing falling into a vat could be dangerous.

Doors and windows

The main door should be wide enough to allow tanks and other large equipment to be brought in, and should open outwards to save valuable space. Windows should be installed at both ends of the plant for good ventilation and should be large enough to allow sufficient air and light to enter to control bacterial growth. Screens on doors and windows keep out insects.

Layout

The layout of the plant should allow for easy access to equipment, maximum convenience and good work-flow. Local engineers and metal-workers can often design and make equipment to a very high standard at a far lower price than imported goods, and should be used as much as possible. Four rooms — the cheese room, maturing room, storeroom and office — and an outside reception area are the factory's minimum requirement and each need different environmental conditions. They should all be on the same level (except in the case of a gravity circuit, see Figure 19), partly to simplify drainage and water disposal, but also because stairs are a great inconvenience (Figure 20).

Reception

As only cheesemakers and assistants should be allowed inside the plant, and to prevent dust and mud from entering, the reception area should be outside the plant, near the cheese room. A concrete platform with a tank and water-tap in the reception area permits easy washing of transport tanks and churns; make sure that water can run off, and not remain as puddles.

64

Cheese processing room

This should be quite a warm room containing the equipment for analysis, pasteurization, cheesemaking and pressing. The tanks should be near the pressing table.

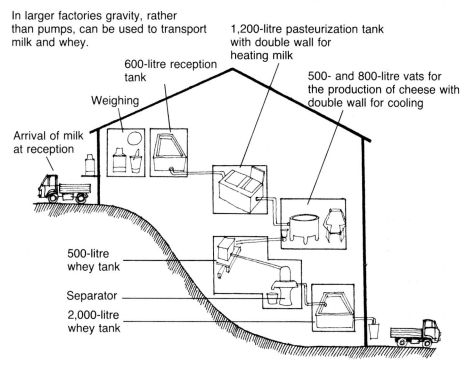

In larger factories gravity, rather than pumps, can be used to transport milk and whey.

1,200-litre pasteurization tank with double wall for heating milk

600-litre reception tank

500- and 800-litre vats for the production of cheese with double wall for cooling

Weighing

Arrival of milk at reception

500-litre whey tank

Separator

2,000-litre whey tank

Figure 19. Gravity circuit of a 2,000-litre cheese factory.

Curing or ripening room

The curing and ripening process is as important as the cheesemaking process. Each type of cheese needs its own specific environment and this book has described Andino, Tilsit, Danbo and Gruyère which require a temperature of between 12 and 15°C and a humidity of 85 to 90 per cent. Very often (even in the most suitable geographical areas), these conditions do not occur naturally throughout the year and in designing cheese factories, it is essential to plan the ripening rooms in the best possible location.

Ripening rooms can be semi earth-sheltered, or installed in old adobe houses with very thick insulating walls. A false ceiling built under the roof insulates the room better. There should be few windows, none receiving a lot of light, and ideally, the room should be protected by

65

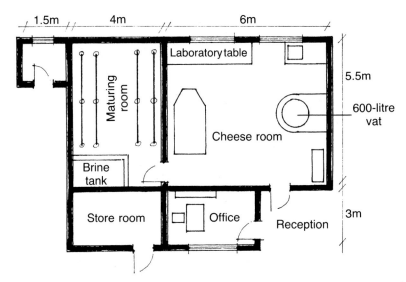

Figure 20. Plan of a 600-litre-capacity cheese factory (scale: 1:75).

trees. The windows can be opened at night, to allow a flow of air if the humidity is too high and strong window screens can be used to prevent insects and animals from entering.

If the humidity drops too low the floor of the ripening room can be flooded with a few centimetres of water to provide the necessary moisture.

Small factories (up to 600 litres of milk a day) need a maturing room of about 5.5 by 4m. There should be long narrow shelves of three-quarter inch galvanized metal water-tubes, which do not rust. The end supports (see Figure 21) can be made of wood, into which horizontal tubes can be easily fitted. Boards to hold the cheeses should be short, light and easily moved, so that they can be taken out, washed, sterilized and replaced by clean dry boards weekly. Almost any kind of wood can be used to make these planks — the less porous, the better — except plywood. Certain very green woods secrete substances that can stain the cheeses. In these cases, first soak the boards in water for several hours and then dry them well.

The brine tank (see Figure 21) can also be located in the maturing room. The size depends on the number of cheeses, but should be about 80cm high and made of cement. To facilitate working with the tank, fill the first 20cm with concrete, the next 30cm with the brine solution, and allow the top 30cm for the increase in volume when the cheeses are added. Incline the bottom slightly towards an outlet that is opened to drain the tank about every two months. Tile the inside and the outside of the tank with durable white tiles which are both inexpensive and easy to

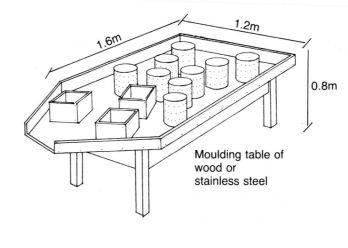

1.6m

1.2m

0.8m

Moulding table of
wood or
stainless steel

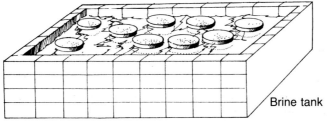

Brine tank

Removable wooden planks —
approximately 0.80 × 0.25m

Galvanized 2cm tubes

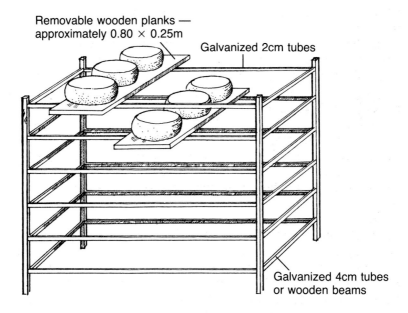

Galvanized 4cm tubes
or wooden beams

Figure 21. Basic equipment for the cheese factory.

67

clean. Because the high moisture and salinity content of the air in the maturing room is detrimental to metal and wood alike nothing else should be located there.

Equipment storage room

The equipment storage room, next door to the maturing room, is used to keep shipping boxes, salt, and various other necessary items. The doorway of the storage room leads to the outside, close to the drying and packing room.

In larger cheese factories (1,000 to 1,500 litres of milk per day) there should be:
○ a curing room — with brine tank and the fresh cheeses up to one-week old;
○ a ripening room — for Andino, Tilsit, Danbo;
○ a ripening room — for Gruyère;
○ a drying and packing room.

Drying and packing room

Just before the cheese is ready to be sold, it is washed with cold water and scrubbed with a soft brush. It is kept in the drying room for one to two days. When it is dry, it is covered with a liquid plastic (Foodplast or Mowilith) which is applied with a sponge. Foodplast or Mowilith are often used, but other forms of polyvinyl acetate are available and waxing or other forms of packaging can be used. The top half is sponged first, left to dry for half a day, then turned over for the bottom half to be sponged. The label is immediately placed on top of the liquid plastic so that it will dry and adhere to the cheese. The cheeses are then weighed and packed, ready to be sold.

Equipment for a 600-litre-capacity cheese factory

Cheese processing

○ Cheesemaking vat (stainless steel, double jacket, 600 litre capacity)
○ Kerosene burner
○ Cheesecutting harp or multi-bladed 'American knives'
○ Wooden paddle
○ Hanging scale
○ 4 plastic buckets
○ Brushes and brooms
○ Water filter
○ 5 40-litre cans (plastic or aluminium)
○ 1 clock
○ 1 plastic scoop
○ 2 thermometers

68

○ Plastic aprons
○ Plastic containers for whey, total capacity of 600 litres
○ Water hose for cleaning
○ Fine cloth to strain the milk (to stretch over the vat)

For moulding the cheese

○ Wooden table (see Figure 21). (Stainless steel is preferable, but costs about 15 times as much).
○ Moulds:
  Tilsit cheese = 25 cylinders of 20cm diameter and 15cm height
  Andino cheese = 70 cylinders of 15cm diameter and 25cm height
  Fresh (white) cheese = 85 cylinders of 10cm diameter and 25cm height (each mould = 2 cheeses)
  Danbo cheese = 13 rectangular pieces of 25 × 25 × 15cm height (made of wood)
  Note: since these moulds are not found on the market we have made our moulds from pieces of drainage pipe made of strong plastic. We cut pieces from the drainage pipe to the measurements indicated, and drill holes of 3mm in diameter at distances of 2cm.
○ 25 wooden discs of 20cm diameter (to fit inside the moulds)
  70 wooden discs of 15cm diameter
  13 wooden covers of 25 × 25cm
  (Note: fresh, white, South American cheese does not need discs)
○ 25 weights of 6 to 8kg measuring 20cm in diameter
  70 weights of 4kg measuring 15cm in diameter
  13 weights of 10kg each (24 × 24cm)
  to fit inside the moulds
○ 2 stainless steel trays with 42 holes each; these are placed over the 42 white cheese moulds, in order to fill them quickly (see p.36).
○ 3m of thick nylon mesh (2mm squares) to place under the moulds.
○ 20m of fine cheesecloth for cutting and rolling each cheese separately.
○ 5m of plastic to cover the cheese in the moulds.

Laboratory

○ table (wooden or built-in)
○ gas stove with two burners
○ wooden incubator to prepare cultures
○ three pots (aluminium) to prepare cultures (15 litres, 10 litres, 5 litres)
○ six plastic containers of one or two litres each, with large neck and lid
○ two big knives to cut cheese
○ milk testing: see pp.17-23
○ Cheese wire-cutters.

69

Ripening room

Shelves: see Figure 21
100 planks of 80 × 25cm
strong table for curing the cheeses
plastic containers for delivering the cheeses

Daily necessities

Rennet, freeze-dried cultures, calcium chloride, salt, detergent, kerosene, gas, plastic bags for fresh (white) cheeses, labels for ripened cheeses, paper for wrapping ripened cheeses, foodplast, brushes, reagents for testing.

Production costs

Unstable exchange rates and unpredictable currency fluctuations make it impossible to provide a set of figures which all readers of this book will find realistic. The following figures, therefore, which are based on production costs in Ecuador in August 1986, are intended to serve only as a guide to the approximate relative outlays required for equipment, materials, and labour.

Soft South American white cheese	Sucres Ecuatorianos[1]
200 litres of milk (18.00 Sucres each)	3,600
5g of rennet powder	76
20g of calcium chloride	20
cultures (2 freeze-dried bags every month)	20
3kg of salt	120
57 plastic bags	102
1 bag of detergent	25
9 litres of kerosene	18
gas	19
labour costs	200
transportation of the cheese to market	31
expenses for the accompanying person	27
depreciation	78
interest (12% per year)	133
other	99
PRODUCTION COSTS	4,568
sale of 57 cheeses at 95 Sucres each[2]	5,425
Profit	856

1. Sucres 165 = US$1
2. 3.5 litres of milk = 1 cheese of 450g The cheese is sold within 3 days, and keeps for a maximum of 7 days in the refrigerator.

Andean Cheese	Sucres Ecuatorianos
200 litres of milk (18.00 Sucres)	3,600
5g of rennet powder	76
10g of calcium chloride	20
2 freeze-dried cultures every month	20
3kg of salt	120
24 labels	41
detergent	25
9 litres of kerosene	18
gas	19
labour	200
transportation of the cheese to Quito	100
accompanying personnel	27
depreciation	78
interest (12% per year)	133
other	99
PRODUCTION COSTS	4,506
sale of 23.5 Andino cheeses (250 Sucres each)[1]	5,876
Profit each day	1,365

1. 8.5 litres of milk = 1 Andino cheese of one kg. The cheese is sold within 10 to 15 days and keeps for several weeks at a temperature of about 15°C.

Key points for successful rural cheesemaking

Milk Production

○ Milk production from the same cows can be increased considerably if the quality and quantity of the feed is high. This can be done by a reasonable use of pasture, including field rotation and even distribution of natural soil fertilizer. It is important to keep individual cow yields and to breed from the best. Pedigree cows only should be bought when adequate handling and balanced feed is assured.

○ Cheesemakers should visit milking stations to encourage care in cleanliness and to test for mastitis. They also need to inform the farmers of the dangers of selling milk that has come from cows which received antibiotics less than five days earlier.

○ Mastitis is controlled basically with careful handling of the cows and hygienic milking. Only in cases of clinical mastitis are antibiotics recommended.

○ The government must be encouraged to sponsor health programmes for cattle and co-operate with vaccination programmes to eradicate bovine brucellosis.

HEALTHY COWS, CLEAN MILKING AND RAPID MILK TRANSPORTATION TO THE CHEESE FACTORY IS THE FORMULA FOR SUCCESS.

From milk to cheese

○ Cheesemakers must analyse the milk upon reception in the cheese plant: smelling, checking colour and hygiene. Density tests must be made twice weekly and reductase tests once a week. The results should be noted regularly and discussed with farmers.
○ The technical process should be recorded daily, so that it can be compared with the final quality of the cheese and eventual problems can be pinpointed.
○ All the equipment as well as the factory itself must be cleaned at the end of each process.
○ Each day the cheesemakers must have enough hot water available so that transporters bringing the milk can immediately wash their containers. All milk buckets have to be checked regularly by the cheesemakers.
○ Cheesemakers must work carefully, so as not to break any utensils, waste milk or curds or use more rennet than is needed to coagulate the milk in 30 to 35 minutes.

Administration

○ The administration must co-ordinate daily activities and responsibilities for each cheesemaker. Since experience only comes after at least three years of work, it is better not to change cheesemakers often.
○ Bookkeeping must be done daily, as well as keeping records of daily production yields. An inventory of materials and an economic balance must be made every three months.
○ Cheesemakers must be paid an appropriate wage, as well as a production incentive bonus.
○ Farmers should be rewarded for excellent milk quality. The result of the processed products depends not only on the experience of the cheesemaking personnel but also on the quality of the milk.

PERSONAL HYGIENE, CLEAN EQUIPMENT AND ORDER IN THE FACTORY ARE INDISPENSABLE FOR HIGH QUALITY PRODUCTS.

Appendices

1. Cheese formulae

Stages of production	Fresh cheese	Andean cheese	Tilsit & Danbo cheese	Parmesan	Gruyère
Quantity of milk	100 litre	100 litre	100 litre	100 litre	330 litre
Coagulation temperature	36°C	33-35°C	32-34°C	31-32°C	32°C
Lactic ferment	0.3 litre	1 litre	1 litre	0.5-1 litre yoghurt	1.5 litre Emmental mix/yoghurt
Coagulation time	30-40 min	30-40 min	30-40 min	30 min	30 min
Cutting and Stirring	10 min	15-25 min	30 min	45 min	30 min
Grain sizes: diameter	2 cm	1½ cm	1 cm	½ cm	½ cm
Repose	3 min	5 min	5 min	5 min	5 min
Whey removed	35 litre	35 litre	35 litre	35 litre	no
Hot water	20 litre	20 litre	20-30 litre	10 litre	no
Water temperature	35°C	50-55°C	65-75°C	80°C	52-55°C
Whey temperature	35°C	37°C	39°C	55°C	50-60 min
Water and Stirring	5 min	10 min	25 min	60-80 min	
Total time	50 min	70 min	90 min	140-160 min	
Mould: diameter	10cm	15cm	25 × 25cm	25cm	38cm
height	25cm	25cm	15cm	15cm	15cm
First turn	yes	yes	yes	yes	yes
Pressing	no	no	6kg	6kg	20kg
Second turn	after 30 min	after 30 min	after 30 min	after 30 min	after 30 min
Pressing	no	4kg	6kg	6kg	200kg
Third turn	after 45 min	after 60 min	after 60 min	after 60 min	after 2 hours
Pressing	no	cut the cheese in two	no	6kg	12 hours with 200kg
Fourth turn	after 80 mins cut each cheese in half and put them quickly into brine	10 hours without weight in moulds (20°C)	10 hours without weight in moulds (20°C)	10 hours without weight	after 2 hours
Brining time	1-2 hrs	8-10 hrs	20-25 hrs	3 weeks	48 hours
Ripening time	0	14 days	4-8 weeks	6-10 months	3-8 months
Yield (litres of milk required per kg of cheese)	7.5 litre	8.5 litre	9.5 litre	12 litre	11 litre
Weight	0.420kg	1kg	2.8/5kg	5kg	30kg

2. Types of dairy cultures

Name	Optimum incubation temperature (°C)	Used for	Characteristics
Emmental-mix	37–42	Emmental, Gruyère, Italian hard cheese	Mixed cultures of *Lactobacillus helveticus* and *Streptococcus thermophilus*
Lactic cultures with aromatizers	20–23	Butter, acidified milk products, cheese	Mixed cultures containing betacoccus and streptococcus acidifiers and aromatizers
Lactic cultures without aromatizers	20–23	Soft cheese and cheese with firm structure	Mixed cultures containing only streptococcus acidifiers (lactis and cremoris)
Leuconostoc citrovorum *Leuconostoc dextranicum*	20–23	Buttermilk, sour cream, cottage cheese, ripened cream butter	Produce only flavour; have to be used together with lactic ferments (*Streptococcus lactis* and/or *Streptococcus cremoris*)
Penicillium camemberti *Penicillium candidum*	15	Camembert cheese	Surface growth with a white mat surface producing a nutty flavour and a creamy texture; it is added directly to the milk
Penicillium roqueforti	10	Blue cheese (Gorgonzola, Roquefort, etc.)	The air induces the mould spores to grow vegetatively with a resulting spread of their greenish-blue mycela, effecting the flavour and texture of the cheese; it is added directly to the milk
Propionibacterium shermanii	28–32	Cheese with eye formation	Grows with difficulty in ordinary milk; added just before the rennet for flavour and eye formation in hard cheese, in addition to Emmental-mix
Streptococcus diacetylactis	30–37	Buttermilk, sour cream, cottage cheese, ripened cream butter	Produces acid and flavour
Streptococcus durans *Streptococcus faecalis*	37–40	Soft Italian cheese, Cheddar and some Swiss cheese	A species of bacteria resistant to salt and heat which imparts a characteristic flavour
Yoghurt	37–42	Yoghurt, hard cheese	Mixed cultures of *Lactobacilus bulgaricus* and *Streptococcus thermophilus*

These starters can be ordered from different laboratories in lyophilized form in small bags or bottles and can be conserved in the refrigerator for about three months. They cost approximately US$5 each.

74